VISNOSTICS™

Special Edition for Real Estate

The Power of
VISualization DiagNOSTIC
Statements
A Neuroscientific Approach to
Communicating, Training, Selling, Marketing, and
Leading.

Kimberlee Slavik

Illustrated by David A. Wiener
Foreword by Denise Fair

DEDICATION

I dedicate all of my books to my wonderful clients for helping me understand how to make sales an honorable, respected, strategic, intelligent, and rewarding process.

SPECIAL THANKS

Thank you to the readers of *Visnostic Selling* for helping it earn Amazon's "Hot New Release in Global Marketing" on the first day it was released!

For all of the innovators and early adopters who had the insight to understand the power of Visnostics, who bravely championed Visnostic Workshops, and who radically changed their company's messaging because of it – THANK YOU & CONGRATULATIONS!

Thanks for the new artwork David! Neither of us could do this without your wonderful wife, Donna's support!

A very special thanks to the owners of ReMax in Waco, TX for sharing such an incredible success story! And Thanks to David Stoltzman for jumping in and writing excellent Visnostics for his real estate business to share in this book!

Scotty, I love you.

And finally, thank you to my son, Zachary Steele Slavik, for designing the cover and helping me find the courage to self publish my first book excerpt! It's so fun being adults together!

VISNOSTICS™ Special Edition for Real Estate

The Power of
VISualization DiagNOSTIC Statements
A Neuroscientific Approach to
Communicating, Training, Selling, Marketing, and Leading.

Copyright © 2019 by Kimberlee Slavik www.dynaexec.com
Illustrations by David A. Wiener

ISBN: 978-1-7331946-1-7
Library of Congress Cataloging-in-Publication is available.
Design & Layout by DynaExec
Published by DynaExec
Cover by Zachary Steele Slavik, CEO of Steele Cross Productions

Printed in the United States of America

VISualization DiagNOSTIC Statements™
Defined

Visualization

verb (used without object)

to recall or form mental images or pictures.

Diagnostic

adjective

of, relating to, or used in diagnosis.

serving to identify or characterize; being a precise indication.

Statement

noun

something stated.

a communication or declaration in speech or writing, setting
forth facts, particulars, etc.

Please note that this is a
Special Edition for Real Estate Agents.
This is an excerpt from *Visnostic Sales and
Marketing* which replaces *Visnostic Selling*.

Table of Contents

FOREWORD

By

Denise Fair,

Owner of RE/MAX Centex in Waco, TX

Each office independently owned and operated.

I have always looked up to Kimberlee and have known her since 1972. She was that girl who always did everything right and seemed to effortlessly excel at everything.

While she may argue with the "effortlessly" part, I did want to be like her when I grew up. My respect for her has grown as I have witnessed her success over obstacles that she encountered and the accomplishments she has achieved.

Readers would be wise to follow her lead, as I have, on how to fully incorporate Visnostics into their businesses. She is a BOSS!

As owner of RE/MAX Centex, I have the opportunity to interact with Buyers, Sellers and other real estate professionals on a daily basis. I have been privileged to experience Kimberlee's passion.

Her Visnostic Statements allow me to *see* from a creative place in my mind...a place I never knew existed!

Since spending time in that newfound creative place, new marketing visions were born. I can NOW say that I am a better real estate agent, a better business owner, a better teacher and a better leader.

I recently used a Visnostic Statement in a pre-listing marketing piece and the results did not disappoint. Rather, my Sellers benefitted in dramatic fashion, selling their home for a 20% premium over asking price within 48 hours of listing it!

My Sellers had the good fortune of entertaining multiple offers, resulting in a seamless closing; the Buyers got the dream home they envisioned (which vision quite probably was influenced by my Visnostic Statement); and of course both real estate agents prospered and relationships developed.

? **Would YOU like to say that you were able to choose from seven offers, all at or above asking price, the first day the house was listed?**

? **Would YOU like to say that your Seller has chosen the best agent for the listing?**

? **Would you like to say your Buyer has chosen the house of their dreams because you helped them envision a happy and rewarding lifestyle in it?**

You CAN say all of these things if you will open your mind and use Visnostic Statements in your marketing.

There is a problem in our industry. Real Estate Agents are using the number of bedrooms and bathrooms to try to sell houses. Clients don't dream of purchasing a three-bedroom, two-bathroom house. Rather, they long to make memories in a home that has a large yard and a pool, perfect for entertaining family and friends on a sunny day. They may envision a home where they can enjoy nights in front of the fireplace when it is cold, or being seated at the kitchen table with the kids enjoying lively conversation and a home-cooked meal. Visnostics helps me sell by giving my clients the "vision thing" which is a pictorial and illustrative suggestion that complements the written word.

Now that I am programmed to think Visnostically (I love using new words!), I think of marketing in a new way. You try it! In addition to imagining enjoying a chilly night in front of the fireplace, now imagine marketing differently with your photographs (this is my favorite part). Let's add people to the photos! Now you see a mom and daughter snuggled in front of the fireplace, reading a book with a fuzzy blanket, flames dancing in the background. WHOA! Do you see what just happened? This is a game changer!

My company, RE/MAX Centex, is the first real estate company on the planet to embrace Visnostics, setting us apart from everyone else. We won't be the last.

I want to thank Kimberlee for sharing her tools with me. I will translate the wisdom contained in the next few pages to assist my fellow agents in growing their businesses and I encourage all readers of this book to do the same.

Proverbs 16:20
"Whoever gives heed to instruction prospers, and blessed is the one who trusts in the LORD."

REVIEWS*

Of

Kimberlee Slavik's Best Selling First Book,

VISNOSTIC SELLING

and

TRANSLATION WORKSHOPS

Comments are from a diverse group of talent and experience including a Teacher, Politician, Visualization Expert, Direct Sales, Solution Architect, Channel Sales, Marketing, Ad Agency, Authors and Buyers. This book is written for everybody.

Investing time to read this section of the book will help open your mind to how Visnostics can be applied in many more areas of your life beyond sales and marketing.

Politicians, teachers, and police officers are just a few examples of readers that are leveraging Visnostics to enjoy amazing results in their respective careers.

"This is a a great read--thought-provoking, engaging and super practical. It really gets to the heart of what great salespeople do naturally, but many average performers and newer reps struggle with: the ability to create a conversation that leads TO their solution, rather than WITH their solution. I'd highly recommend Kimberlee Slavik's terrific book to anybody looking to take their selling approach to the next level."

-Matthew Dixon, coauthor of The Challenger Sale, The Challenger Customer and The Effortless Experience

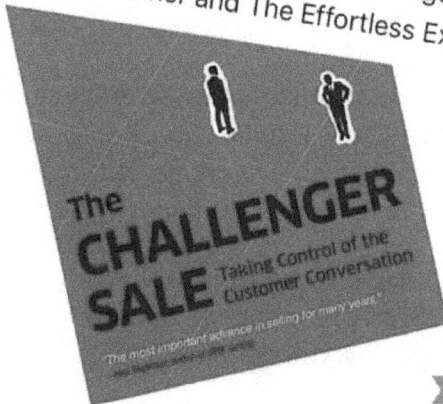

The CHALLENGER SALE Taking Control of the Customer Conversation

"The most important advance in selling for many years."

PIC·COLLAGE

Jennifer, Sales Channel Marketing & Sales Executive for a Fortune 500 Company (Top 60 with $28 Billion in annual revenue)

"With Kim's help we have been able to shift our focus from educating the customer about a specific product to identifying gaps in a customers desired end state and focus our attention on their needs versus our speeds & feeds. The Visnostic Statement method is a powerful tool to get your customers excited about the benefits without ever mentioning the products and services. It's ingenious – easy for sellers as they are simply getting to know their customer better and easy for customers because we are not asking them to make the connections between our offerings and their environment."

"As I read 'Visnostic Selling' a light bulb went off in my head; we had been doing it all wrong. No wonder the message wasn't resonating with customers, we were starting with meeting 3. By working with Kim to translate our "Meeting 3" marketing presentation into Visnostics Statements suitable for a first meeting with the customer, we are able to "diagnose" the customer and cater subsequent presentations to their specific needs (that we learn through the visnostic statement scoring). It's brilliant! We've turned a first meeting monologue into an engaging dialogue. Sellers love it. Customers love it. We are making it EASY and engaging for everyone. Thank you Kim! "

David Wiener, Senior Sales Leader

"During my selling career of 50 years, I read all the sales books and even taught some. I believe the perceived needs of the customer and the apparent solutions to these needs have always controlled the relationship between seller and buyer. This, the weakest point in the sales cycle has never been fully addressed until now.

For the last ten years, Kim Slavik has worked on a method for establishing the real customer needs and their priorities. She has also created an easily understood way of establishing and presenting these needs and priorities.

Visualization Diagnostic Statements will change the way selling is performed. It is a win-win for buyer and seller. I am honored to have worked with Kim and illustrated her book."

Sherry Hall, Award-Winning Author, and Educator
"While Kim's work most certainly has the potential to be life-changing for salespeople, it also holds implications beyond the world of business. As an educator, I have seen first hand the power of visualization. I believe Kim's groundbreaking book can create positive change across multiple settings."

Phil White former Sales VP, Computer Associates
"A refreshing common-sense approach of engaging customers and prospects from their perspective. A must read for any modern-day sales organization."

James "Jim" Hester, Solution Architect, Pre and Post Sales Support
"As a pre-sales solution architect with decades of industry experience, I've noticed certain characteristics that make sales teams more successful than others. A successful sales team must listen more than they speak and absorb everything they see and hear. Although you might think I'm spelling out "Solution Selling," after reading Kim's innovative book you will find that products coupled together do not yield a solution and customers know it. Customers want to differentiate their products and services to their customers but before they can their vendors and partners must listen, prioritize, and gain acceptance of future directions. It is too often assumed that we (as salespeople) truly understand the customer's business

almost without any interaction; after all we have a solution for everything. Building and interpreting Visnostic Statements will accelerate a longer, more valued relationship with your customers putting you in the "trusted advisor" driver's seat."

Omar Barraza, Marketing Expert, Founder of PlanStartGrow™, and creator of Almost Free Marketing™

"Kim's book is the most effective manifesto for revealing the intrinsic value of genuinely understanding a person's professional and personal needs, wants, and expectations. And while her book is destined to become a 'best seller' among resourceful sales professionals, I think it is a 'must read' for anyone in marketing interested in finding new ways to communicate more precisely, accurately, and effectively with past, present and future customers and clients. That's why we now incorporate the principles of Kim's innovative creation when introducing Almost Free Marketing™ and advise our clients to leverage Visnostic Statements too."

Pamela Luke, MBA, Sales and Marketing Professional

"This powerful book is chock-full of brilliant non-conventional sales and marketing advice on so many levels. One point of value applicable to many industries is the marketing team may never be in a position to purchase the product their company manufactures. Yet, they are required to produce material that will capture the market. This requires a combination of ingenuity and great salesmanship to clinch the deal. Kim takes the reader seamlessly through the steps needed to make the "sell" genuine in order to win while offering positive and engaging motivation."

Commander & Lieutenant
Senior Buyers for the Police Department

"Personally having no distinct sales background in marketing or technology, a company recently came in to present their

offering of an internet platform they built to show how it could improve work in my field, as I represented a local municipality. I was interested in the concept and eager to see if I thought their product could improve our data collection, as were fifteen other decision makers sitting in the room. Five minutes after they started their PowerPoint presentation I thought to myself "I'm not engaged in this. I do not see why it is important to have this". Ten minutes later looking around the room multiple others had begun checking their phones or otherwise checking out. I had recently read a draft of Kim's book and had multiple conversations with her on Visnostic Statements and the benefits of engaging listeners (clients) in visualization and true feedback. As a consumer or customer I feel I have a better understanding of what to expect from a product or sales meeting and if the person who says they can provide it, really understands my needs and how their product can fulfill them.

I wish this company had read this book or spoken with Kim on truthfully and honestly engaging with the client or end user to prepare their presentation. The presenter did have a valid product they were trying to bring to the market but most likely could have improved market buy in thousands of times faster and more successfully if they had the knowledge this author or her methods bring to the table. "

Bridget Cogley, Tableau Zen Master & Visualization Expert

"We can automate so much. What we can't automate is the human connection, the relationships we build and the novel - and very human - solutions we improvise. Kimberlee understands this, humanizing data and using it to find success in a manner that proves itself time and time again. So, use it to change sales, but use it elsewhere too. Where do you need to build connection and convince others?

Visnostic Selling gets to the heart of what clients want - not just what businesses want to throw at them. It lets prospects share their values, deepest dreams, and hopes, so that you - a fellow human - can bond and see a shared path in a way that no automation can provide. You know the potential solution and path your business can provide. What are often missing are the unique gaps clients see, fear, and want to correct. Kimberlee provides a system that's human-centric, allowing us to bypass jargon that's cluttered the path to understanding to get to the root of what clients need. It builds success in a way that's transformational, sustainable, and wildly successful.

Use this book to bond and to transform the process so the client shines, you support them on their path, and trust becomes the norm. Expand by letting this process become a longitudinal benchmark, allowing you to return, re-prioritize, and reach new heights with clients. Intuition and data-driven decision-making can work together."

Carolynn Boss, Senior Vice President of Sales and Business Development

"Having been in Sales more than half of my career, I wish that someone had shared this unique way of approaching a client before. I've been successful in my career but I could have done so much more. So many times I was forced to use the Company presentation that spent 30-60 minutes bragging about the size and importance of the company I was working for and then went into deep heavy-duty product descriptions that could literally put a client to sleep. Visualization Diagnostic Statements allows the client to be able to understand the benefits he would derive from your technology, understand how it will help his company (and even his career progression when he makes a great decision), while creating an almost automatic sponsor for you while

doing it. Sometimes we just need to dare to be different. I find myself looking for the Visualization Diagnostic Statements that should be used for every sales conversation now."

Kelly, Account Representative, Ad Agency ($697 Million in annual revenue)

"The concept of Visnostic Statements has truly revolutionized the way I help my clients develop messaging for their brand. Kim's workshop encouraged my clients to recognize the importance of adopting a customer-centric strategy, which will help their brand resonate with prospective customers and ultimately increase sales of their products."

Harrison, Regional Sales Manager for Fortune 100 Company

"Kim's Visualization Diagnostic Statements will give my team of new sellers a scientific method for how to create content & communicate their company's value to customers. The power in Kim's methodology for my team comes from its simplicity, relatability & ease of deployment in their day-to-day.

As a management tool it helps to show where each reps' strengths & weaknesses are so I can continue to develop my people as effectively as possible. Thanks to Kim, my team & I will be more confident in communicating our value to customers."

Lynda Stokes, Politician and Former Mayor of Reno, TX

"Kimberlee Slavik has done a masterful job in explaining the art of communication/sales through neuroscience.

Reading her book is as easy as having coffee with a friend. The stories in this book and the Individual exercises help us to better understand our own thought process in order to communicate with others. As a politician I know we have just a few seconds to grab someone's attention. Kim's book will help you break through the walls we all build. In the business world I am constantly challenged to put myself out there as a product to others. This book is giving me insight and tools to build a vision and the ability to develop visions in others. Therefore, better fulfilling their needs. Putting this into play can pull somebody from the bottom of the barrel and put him or her at the top of the mountain.

INTRODUCTION
The Science of VISNOSTICS
WHY/HOW/WHAT

WHY you want to read this book

Once upon a time, there was a mother and daughter. One gorgeous afternoon, these lovely women were carrying on a family tradition of cooking a prize-winning roast. The recipe was a closely guarded secret and had been in their family for decades. However, the recipe was extremely precise. The roast had to be an exact weight, the spices had to be carefully measured, the meat had to marinate for a specific amount of time, and even the weather had to be just right for the oven to work its magic.

One day as the mother was teaching all the secrets to the daughter, the roast was properly prepared and it was ready to be put into the pan. Suddenly, the mother pulled out a cutting board and cut the end of the roast off. The daughter was confused and asked the mother why she did that. The mother scratched her head and said, "I honestly don't know. This is how my mother taught me to do it. Let me call her and ask."

The mother called the matriarch and described how perfectly the roast preparation had gone and then asked for the reason they cut off the end of the roast before cooking. The elder mother burst out laughing and said, "Well Honey, I don't know why YOU did it but my pan was too small! "

I absolutely love this story because we have all been guilty of this behavior in some form or fashion during our lives. We tend to do things because it was the way they were always done. Every once in a while, we will stop and ponder why we do it and if it can be done differently.

If I could summarize this book, this is it. You are about to learn how to do something VERY unique but there is powerful science behind why it works and why you should have been doing it this way your entire life!

In fact, you are about to embark on a journey that will change everything you thought you knew about marketing and sales. Once you have finished this book, you will be armed with powerful knowledge and insight that will inspire you to do things very differently from the way you do them today.

If this book accomplishes what is intended, you will want to review and enhance your current messaging. Visnostics will make your message much more meaningful, impactful, and memorable to your audience.

It will also change the way you purchase things because your expectations will change with how you view a sales process. As a Buyer, you will ask better questions during the purchasing and exploration process.

Your message will be reconstructed to inspire your audience. You will transform your presentations with fewer words and better visuals to ensure your audience remembers your message. They will want to engage with you and share important strengths and weaknesses with you. You will be amazed as your audience becomes enthusiastic about what you have to offer them and their company.

You will NOT be asking questions. You will be making a statement that triggers visualization. And visualization often triggers emotions. The result will be that your audience will give you more information than typically given after a question. And they will ENJOY this new approach!

People don't just buy from people they like;
they buy because they become emotional
about the potential solutions
and the people from whom they buy.

You will experience for yourself how one simple word can trigger many different emotions and visualizations. Knowing and seeing this will help you ensure you validate your audiences' interpretations of your words. You will become aware of how our brains avoid work and how this avoidance keeps sales and clients out of sync with one another. However, you will also learn how to ensure this isn't a problem in the future.

You will learn the importance of translating your offerings into a language and delivery to which your clients can relate. You will see how this translation step strengthens your relationship with your clients because they will be grateful that you will take this translation burden off their shoulders. You will learn how to take data from your clients and translate that data into valuable information that they can use to sell you and your capabilities internally. You will learn how to create your own tools that will aid in translating pains, weaknesses, challenges, and strengths into an insightful and powerful deliverable for your client. Subsequently, you will change your life, your clients' lives, and the lives of the people around you with this new knowledge and skill!

You will change your life, your clients' lives,
and the lives of the people around you with
this new knowledge and skill!

WHY & HOW this book is written

RUSSIAN NESTING DOLLS

Simon Sinek's book *Start With Why* is one of the most-watched Ted Talks of all time with millions of views, and dozens of spin-offs. Sinek created a drawing of three circles with "Why" being the middle starting point. He explains that most companies go right into WHAT they do but they should really start by explaining, "WHY they do what they do." A company should begin each presentation with the purpose and motivation behind what they believe.

The second outer circle should address their process and explain the specific actions they take to support the "WHY." This second step answers HOW they will do what they do.

Finally, the outer most circle and third step should explain WHAT they do. This is when the result of the WHY is explained. Simon Sinek refers to these three steps as "The Golden Circles."

However, when the artist of this book saw the circles, he envisioned that those circles were an aerial view of a Russian Nesting Doll.

For those who don't know what that is, it is a small doll that fits inside a medium doll, that fits inside a large doll. Because visualizations are a critical part of neuroscience, this graphic should help you remember the order in which this thought process flows: Why, How, and What.

I will attempt to follow Simon Sinek's thought process and this Introduction will explain **WHY** I am writing this book, **WHY** you will want to read it, **HOW** you can maximize your benefits and retention of the content, **HOW** you will execute, and **WHAT** you can do to immediately increase your income.

While this is intended to be a stand-alone reference guide, some prerequisite work will help you be much more passionate about what you are about to learn. To truly appreciate and comprehend the content, it will be incredibly helpful for you to understand the basics of Sinek's *Start With Why* because it is full of fundamental details about how the brain works chemically.

After you finish that research, look into *The Challenger Sale* by Matthew Dixon and Brent Adamson, which does an incredible job of explaining why most salespeople never get that important second meeting. It also teaches how to bring true value during your client meetings, which will guarantee that next step in the sales cycle.

Clients want you to paint
a vision of how their lives
and companies could be
better in the future with your help.

It also does a fantastic job explaining why relationship selling (alone) is not as impactful as previously taught. It explains how to address that so it is actually the most impactful sales approach when combined with the Challenger style.

Finally, please read *What Great Salespeople Do* by Michael Bosworth and Ben Zoldan. It basically explains why *The Bible* is the best-selling book of all times; it is full of stories, and our brains LOVE stories! It teaches how to craft your stories to maximize the impact on your audience. Bosworth's book made so many light bulbs go off in my head that it was blinding.

It felt amazing when I finally realized that my success wasn't just dumb luck or good timing! I had been discounting my abilities for years. Once I understood WHY this worked, I became eager to get BETTER at what I was doing!

I finally understood the science behind
some of the strange things I had to do
to get my clients to understand
how I was going to help them.

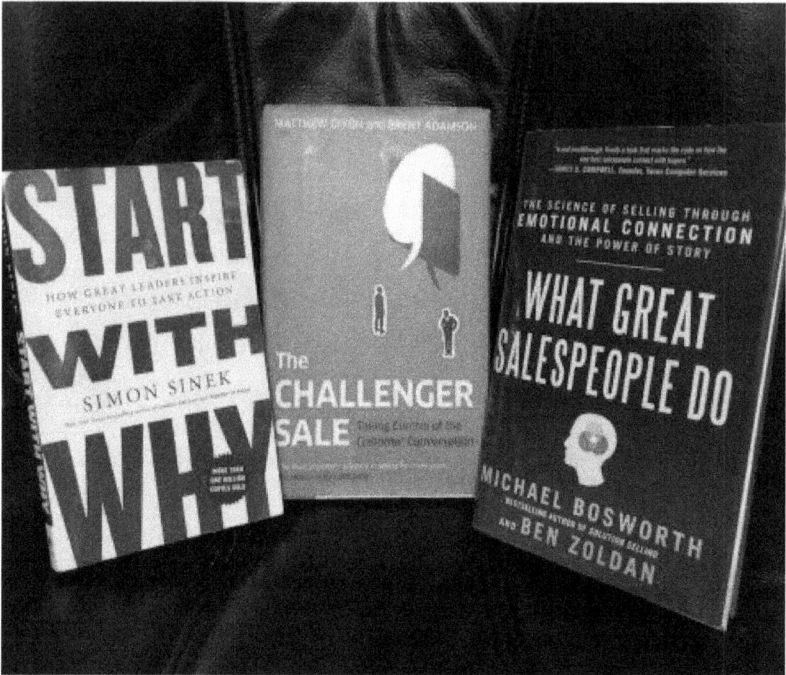

All three of these recommended books are incredible reading by themselves. However, when you combine and execute all three principles, you will harness the most powerful communication approach you have ever seen.

You must help your audience visualize how their life could be better in the future with your help.

The Science of Visnostics

Neuroscience is not just beneficial during a sales process; it is also useful in all the relationships in your life. But the value I want to provide to each reader is a detailed description of specific ways you can take the science described, convert what marketing has already created for you, and go deliver the message in a way that your clients want and need you to deliver it!

Basic sales training will teach you to avoid closed-ended questions but sales training never explains WHY. The chemistry in your brain reacts very differently when asked a question requiring a yes or no answer than when it is asked a question that forces a visualization to occur. An example would be:

Closed-Ended Question – *'Is your car blue?'*
A non-emotional cognitive/cerebral response is triggered.

Visualization Question – *'What color is your car?'*
A visualization is triggered as they see their car in their thoughts, which will cause a much more emotional response.

Rapport is established during emotional responses, not cerebral ones. It is much easier to resist any decision making when emotions are not engaged.

Did you know that the second question momentarily hijacked your thought process and focused it entirely on your car? This is an automatic response. To see this in action, be sure and do the first exercise. As you read this book, it's designed to help build your own confidence and belief in the power of the science behind Visnostics. This is why the exercises exist.

A closed-ended question requires a cerebral response and a visualization question requires a more emotional response. As sales or marketing professionals, we have been taught that people make emotional decisions much easier than a cerebral one. Emotions create a sense of urgency and a cerebral one can take you down a lengthy sales cycle resulting in the dreaded analysis paralysis.

I will review fundamental principles that you probably already know. However, what is very different with Visnostics is you will learn how to trigger powerful chemicals in the brain that will bond you with your audience like nothing you have ever experienced in the past!

When done correctly, you won't be asking a question; you will be making a statement.

Visnostic Statements force the brain to work harder to respond. This process hijacks the brain and becomes one of the most powerful and profound emotional interactions you can have with another human being during a sales process.

I've worked with several Neuroscientists to ensure accuracy with this content and I have been told my books simplify a very complex subject so everybody can understand it.

While many sales training programs focus on the cognitive and emotional aspects of the selling process, Visnostics have brought the power of the meta-cognitive to the world of sales training.

What is meta-cognitive? Metacognition refers to our awareness of and ability to regulate our own thinking. Metacognition might be the self-awareness you have around memorization. When you acknowledge that you have difficulty remembering people's names in social situations, you are engaging your metacognitive understanding of yourself.

Now imagine triggering the metacognitive awareness in your clients! Instead of relying on them to translate your features and functions into how they will benefit, you will guide them through the translation process!

I know that makes very little sense to you right now but as you go through the first few chapters of this book, you will comprehend the power of Visualization Diagnostic STATEMENTS versus questions.

By using Visnostic Statements, you will be able to bring the client's wants and wishes to the surface thus avoiding miscommunication. Furthermore, you will now have the power to get the client emotionally engaged within those critical first few seconds!

While this chapter was being written, I was a guest on a very popular sales podcast. First of all, I loved the interview and was honored to be his guest. But I was mortified when I saw that he named the podcast something like *"Use this type of QUESTION to win deals!"* **VISNOSTIC STATEMENTS ARE NOT QUESTIONS!!!!!** As I listened to the recording, I realized that he actually edited out all of my comments about how questions are not effective. So it was no surprise that his commentary after my interview focused on selling his training around questioning!

Despite what you may have been taught, questioning isn't the Holy Grail to understanding client needs.

Consultative Selling was all the rage in the early 2000's and I took about a dozen different classes on how to ask questions to qualify my clients' needs. However, when I was attempting to execute the questioning principles, I could FEEL my clients getting annoyed. Think about this – when you are on the phone with a support person, they will usually ask you to take a short survey after the call. Do you actually take the time to do them? I worked for a Customer Experience Company and I can tell you that the surveys are rarely done.

Have you ever walked through a mall and someone with a clipboard tried to get you to take a quick survey? Are you excited to do it? Personally, I want to chew a body part off to escape. This desire to resist surveys is also triggered when we blast our clients with a barrage of questions.

Visnostics will teach you about the natural instincts we all have around "Fight or Flight." Questioning will absolutely trigger these resistance responses. Visnostic Statements are a better way to get the answers you need without actually asking questions!! And your clients will appreciate this new approach.

What if you could learn a communication style that would release serotonin in your client's brain versus the Fight or Flight response as you spoke?

This is what Wikipedia says about serotonin - *As a neurotransmitter, serotonin helps to relay messages from one area of the brain to another. ... This includes brain cells related to mood, sexual desire and function, appetite, sleep, memory and learning, temperature regulation, and some social behavior.*

The power in triggering serotonin in your clients' brains is very similar to Pavlov's Dog. Just as Pavlov conditioned a dog to salivate every time he rang a bell, your clients will relate good feelings when they think of YOU.

Triggering the release of serotonin is an incredible way to establish respect, rapport, and credibility instantly!

WHY this book has more graphics and fewer words than most business books

Look closely at this graphic. Did you know that our attention spans are getting shorter at an alarming rate?

In 2000, you had twelve seconds to grab the attention of your audience. In 2015, you only had eight seconds! To put that into perspective, a goldfish has a nine-second attention span. That means that a goldfish will pay attention longer than a human today!

The same year this book was published, the first class of "Generation Z" entered the workforce. Studies have shown that this generation has a THREE-SECOND attention span! That means that your first three words of your message MUST appeal to the reader instantly.

I have worked with enough salespeople to tell you that I highly suspect the typical salesperson has an even lower attention span than a typical human!

With that in mind, the average business book has over 70,000 words and few graphics, each of my books will have less than 35,000 words and several dozen graphics. **Why** am I doing that? Because I want every reader to actually finish reading the entire contents in one sitting AND the pictures will help readers remember the content!

In addition to these books with just 35,000 words and less than 200 pages, I will also be co-writing Visnostic "Special Editions" with experts in specific fields. These books will be about half the size because the focus will be on specific industries.

The goal is that readers will execute and receive an immediate value on a topic very important to them. Once they see the power of Visnostics, they will want to read the complete book so they can become more advanced in these very powerful new skills.

I once read that a study was conducted on college students attending the same class, learning from the same books, the same instructor, and taking the same tests. However, one group did better than the other. The only difference was that one group attended classes Monday, Wednesday, and Friday for one hour each day. The other group attended Tuesday and Thursday for one hour and thirty minutes each day. The study concluded that the shorter the instruction, the better the retention. I'm not sure if this is true or not, but it's another data point to support my strategy of using fewer words by leveraging more visuals.

"You are Who You Are, Because of Where You Were, When" is one of my all-time favorite quotes by Dr. Morris Massey. I recommend that you familiarize yourself with this concept. Entire books have been written on this subject so we won't be able to spend much time dissecting it. However, understanding this concept will enhance your ability to have empathy for your audience. If you understand the basic concept and the importance of adapting to your audience, you will be even better at learning this new communication process. Here is a URL to help you quickly grasp the primary points of this theory – It is a video from the '80s but if you listen closely, you will realize why it's age makes the message even more impactful.

https://www.youtube.com/watch?v=_aY163kwlW4

From my perspective, I love to learn and I love to try new things. Therefore, throughout my career, I embraced the latest sales training that came out. While each book or training course was incredible, and I always learned something new from each one, I also scratched my head in bewilderment. Don't writers know that most salespeople have an incredibly short attention span? Why are books so long? And why are they full of so much 'filler'? When am I supposed to have time to read all these books? Do publishers demand a certain number of pages or words to legitimize the content?

Well, here is the reality of MY world as an eager reader and student – I would get a new book, enthusiastically start reading and by about the fifth chapter, life disrupted my reading and I had to put down the book. A few days or even weeks later, when I got back to the book, I would feel the need to scan the first chapters again to get my head back in the game.

I have dozens of business books in my office and even more audiobooks on various devices. I bet I have read or listened to the first five chapters dozens of times. Sadly, I usually finished them only once! I'm embarrassed to admit this, but I am pretty sure that I have a couple of fantastic books that I never even finished! So why do that to someone else?

The goal is that with less than 35,000 words, you will read each of my books in one sitting; this should increase the probability that you take your excitement and execute while it is fresh in your memory.

In fact, I plan on having you execute in Chapter ONE so not only will you see first hand the power of neuroscience, you will have the confidence to do it TODAY! I also want you to believe in what you are reading. The exercises are critical so you can see these concepts work instantly. As each point is proven to you, you will become more passionate about leveraging these new skills immediately.

WHY exercises will help you learn and retain and execute more effectively

Most of you have probably seen versions of this graphic throughout your career. Which means you all should know that your ability to retain what you learn is maximized when you 'teach' the materials. Therefore, as you read, you will notice multiple exercises that are intended to simulate a teaching scenario that will enhance your comprehension.

Unfortunately, per neuroscience and human nature, you will be tempted to skip the exercises. Even though doing the exercises with other people will increase your ability to remember and comprehend the content, you will convince yourself that you are special and don't need this enhancement for adequate learning. Fight this urge!

Why waste your time reading this book if you only retain 10% of what you read? Doing each exercise will ensure you not only read, but also, hear, see, discuss, experience, and teach. By retaining 95% of what is in the book, you will not waste your valuable time reading a book that you won't remember and you will be more prepared to actually execute these powerful new skillsets!

WHY Graphics are powerful

I also want to explain **why** there is a need for so many graphics. As I shared a draft of this book, I was thrilled how many people gave feedback by referring to the graphics associated with the content. Graphics help the reader retain the information!

Take a look at your current presentations and websites. Do you have more words than pictures? Do your graphics compliment your words? If not, this needs to change immediately. When graphics and words don't complement each other, it confuses the audience. This confusion will cause them to disengage.

Recently I read an article on LinkedIn by Inc. called **"7 Presentation Ideas That Work for Any Topic."** https://www.inc.com/carmine-gallo/7-presentation-ideas-that-work-for-any-topic.html

First of all, I agree with every single word in this article, but I questioned the author as I read it because it instructed the reader to use more pictures than words. Yet there were no pictures. It said to avoid bullets but each point was numbered AND there were bullets. In my opinion, a bullet and a number are the same things. This made the article seem somewhat hypocritical to me and it is important that I don't do that to my readers.

My point here is that I am going to teach you how to do things and I am going to "lead by example" as much as possible. In fact, if you catch me falling short, be sure to communicate your observations with me so I can fix it in future releases! It is so easy to read HOW to do something, but it is a much bigger challenge to go out there and actually execute what you learned!

How can an author legitimize the content if the advice is not followed during the instruction?

Therefore, you will notice that almost every page will have at least one photo or graphic highlighting a point made in the content. This serves multiple purposes. I want you to remember the content but I also want you to find what you are looking for when you need to go back and reference, re-read, or find something.

These points are not intended to instruct you how I am writing a book; they are intended to inspire you to follow this same logic when creating communications with your clients.

I have so many random facts in my head, yet I am challenged to remember who said it or from what book it came. My goal is that while you visualize the artwork, you will remember the content, and be able to quickly reference what you need in the future.

Furthermore, as I travel, teach, and present this methodology, the graphics will replace most of the words and become the focal point of my presentations to improve the retention of the content.

Visualization is a major part of the power of neuroscience.

You will also notice repetition as you read. Studies have uncovered that the mind has to absorb information multiple times and multiple ways to comprehend and retain the concept. So if you find yourself reading something familiar yet a little different, this has been done intentionally to help you retain the content.

The importance of two-way communications

As you look at these two drawings, imagine you are one of the characters in each scene. Which drawing seems to represent the most pleasant form of communication? Do you prefer to be in listen mode or do you prefer to be engaged in the communication process?

Pause as you look at these two scenes and dissect why you chose one over the other. Why is two-way communication scenario so much more attractive than a one-way communication scenario? Why do some people struggle with reading? Which scene is most like reading a book? Isn't reading similar to listening mode? Why do we need classrooms if we can just read books and learn the content?

One of the Visnostic Readers wrote me and told me about a recent graduation commencement speech and he asked his nephew what he thought of the speaker. The response was that the speech was long and boring. Isn't that what we each remember about our own graduations? Can you recall anything that was said? Can you recall the topic? Do you realize it was a one-way-communication? It was long, painful, boring, and unmemorable. Do we really want this same effect on our clients? I know I don't want it to happen to my readers!

Have you ever read an interactive book? I don't think I have! I am sure they exist but they are most certainly in short supply. This is interesting because we are taught in neuroscience that one-way communications are not stimulating and they are unnatural.

Therefore, I will be asking you to do some exercises and to email me your stories. This may seem like a silly thing to do, but it will help you retain what you learned. It will also help you to visualize the emotions you just witnessed. It will be a good experience for you so you will be prepared to convert these approaches to your work life. The ultimate goal is that you will increase your pipeline immediately.

How much you get out of this book is up to you and is dependent upon how well you follow these instructions.

WHAT are Visualization Diagnostic Statements™?
NOTE - Also referred to as a VDS, Diagnostic Statement, or Visnostic in this book.

Visnostic Statements and Visualization Diagnostic Statements are trademarked terms created by Kimberlee Slavik, CEO of DynaExec. They are statements that require a response from an audience. They stimulate emotional responses inspiring your audience to maximize their interest in your message. Visualization Diagnostic Statement is the scientific term. However, readers may want to refer to it by a term more in alignment with their specific business and client base.

The statements typically <u>translate</u> features and functions into something more meaningful to the audience.

A Visnostic Statement often originates as an ineffective, generic, one-way **self-focused** message that has been converted into a meaningful two-way engaging statement that is **audience-focused**. Existing presentations, brochures, case studies, and other marketing materials are often reworded to become Visnostic Statements.

A Visnostic Statement is also a qualification tool that will help you assess your audience. As you go through the statements, if your participant isn't responding or is struggling with responding, chances are high that you aren't in front of the right participant.

A Visnostic Statement is also an effective way to determine if sales and marketing currently have the right messaging. If creating these statements feels effortless, the current messaging is strong. When these statements are difficult to create, the content doesn't contain what the clients need and want to know.

Visnostic Statements will change the way you think. For example, I was helping a reader improve his resume and I commented that there were no results mentioned. He argued that his job didn't produce any results from his efforts. I challenged him to go research some statistics. This young man was in a support role and his relationship with the client was after a sale was completed. He enthusiastically called me back a few days later to tell me that the account he helped, paid the company over 1.5 million dollars annually. He concluded that if he didn't do a good job providing support, the company would lose that revenue stream. He now realizes his value to the company thanks to the research needed to develop Visnostic Statements.

The Importance of A Diagnostic Approach
Cause versus Symptom

I recently participated in a group interview for a sales leadership role. Several people described things they saw as broken in the sales organization and they asked me how I would fix these problems. The complaints ranged from sales were down to morale was low. My response to them was that they were describing a symptom and asking me how to eliminate the pain before I understood the cause of that pain. For my response, I used the analogy of a headache and how a physician would handle a patient with the same dilemma.

Prescribing a painkiller to help the headache go away will not address the cause of the pain; it will only temporarily mask the symptom. I continued by explaining that multiple things could cause a headache such as allergies, caffeine withdrawal, vision problems, medications, a hangover, hormones, a brain tumor, just to name a few. Yet each cause of these pains must be treated very differently to eliminate the SOURCE of the pain.

Just as a good doctor will dig deeper and run tests to determine the cause of the pain, a good salesperson or sales leader should also investigate to ensure he or she is addressing the correct cause of the issues. For example, I typically interview people, review reports, analyze the competitive marketplace, and examine existing business tools in order to uncover the cause of the problem.

Too often enthusiastic and new sales professionals will start attempting to fix the symptom versus taking the necessary extra time to uncover the cause of the issues. This happens with internal pains as well as client pains.

Not until a successful diagnosis of the **cause** of the pain is made, can the appropriate plan of action be executed to eliminate the **source** of the pain.

Visnostic Statements should be constructed to identify your clients' pains and the cause of their pains. It is the responsibility of the sales organization to differentiate pains, challenges, and weaknesses as either causes or symptoms.

Converting typical sales points into this unique format will engage your client and create the desire to share important details that will help properly diagnose the cause and how the client can be helped.

Why This Is Relevant and Important

If a salesperson is taught a presentation and delivers the presentation on sales calls, do they really understand the client's source of the pain?

Converting marketing content into "Visnostic Statements" is the first step in creating a powerful tool that will help diagnose the most effective areas in which the sales team can help the client. Visnostic Statements will create an environment that will stimulate meaningful and valuable conversations with the client.

WHAT Buyers Learn

I knew this book would benefit sales professionals, marketing teams, sales leaders, and any other client-facing roles in an organization. I never envisioned that BUYERS would find the content of value. However, as I was having close friends and family review the draft, I received some unexpected feedback from two people with zero sales backgrounds. While they didn't sell for a living, they did have frequent purchasing requirements and were often forced to endure some pretty tough and painful sales presentations.

I was excited to hear that a few weeks after reading a draft, a very important sales presentation was conducted. People that had a vested interest in learning more about the offering attended the meeting. These two people just happened to be in the same presentation and they told me they viewed the salespeople very differently after learning about the concepts around Visnostic Statements.

They explained that they were on opposite sides of the room, texting each other about how horrible the slides were. They were full of words and bullets and had very few graphics that made sense. They looked around the room and observed the entire audience was disengaged and on their various smart devices. The salespeople had lost the interest of the entire room and now my two friends understood why the presentation was not effective!

These two people went on to explain that they are stronger and more educated buyers after reading the draft. They continued explaining that their expectations are higher than they were before reading the book. They also suggested that I reach out to the company that presented to them because they actually want to buy the offering. However, the salespeople simply didn't build a strong enough case to justify the purchase! This is such terrific insight from Buyers! Therefore, try and imagine how your clients would react to the content you are reading. What would YOUR clients say about YOUR interaction with them?

VDS are Universally Effective

Even though my career has been primarily associated with Silicon Valley companies, Visnostic Statements should apply to all sales and marketing scenarios. For example, if you are a Real Estate Agent and you sell houses based upon the number of bedrooms, bathrooms, square footage, and price, you will sell more if you lead with the real reason clients actually buy homes. One of the greatest Agents I ever worked with told me that she didn't sell homes; she sold dreams. Creating effective VDS will flush out those dreams.

I'm also working with a paint company that insists their buyers buy on price and relationships. They believe that all of their Buyers consider paint to be a commodity. My response to this comment was, "**If your clients view your offerings as a commodity, you are SELLING it as a commodity; VDS will highlight the differentiators that will help change this perspective.**"

To summarize this introduction, you now know WHY this book was written, why you should follow the instructions, and why it is formatted in an unusual way. You also now understand HOW to get the most out of what you read, and WHAT the outcome should be for you, your company, and your clients.

41

CHAPTER ONE
Believing is doing
The Birth of Visualization Diagnostic Statements

n 2004 I represented a company and a service that I was so passionate about that I invested in the company. I sincerely believed that I had ten-dollar bills for sale for just one dollar.

Think about that! If someone gave you a stack of ten-dollar bills and told you that they would pay you commissions to go sell them for one dollar, wouldn't you call every person you knew? Wouldn't you jump out of bed in the morning and go on sales calls with tremendous enthusiasm? I was setting up at least five meetings each day and I would have done more but I ran out of daylight. I still hold sales records at that company! That was my life for the first decade of my career and I sincerely believed that my customers loved me for educating them on what I was selling.

However, there was this one client that shocked and frustrated me because he didn't seem to see the value I brought to him and his company. This is the story of how Visualization Diagnostic Statements were born.

The first time I presented to him, he fell asleep. HE FELL ASLEEP! Of course, he was embarrassed and set up another meeting. I was actually encouraged during the second meeting because I noticed him taking very vigorous notes. He seemed to be really concentrating and really into what he was writing down. I walked over to him and he was doing his grocery list. HE WAS DOING HIS GROCERY LIST!

shopping list

produce	dairy	dry
apples	yogurt	peanut butter
bananas	butter	canned tomato
lemons	eggs	pasta
spinach	keifer	black beans
kale		
celery		
cucumber	meat	misc
yams	chicken	t.p.
red onion		la croix
garlic		laundry det.

I was young and so bewildered that someone wasn't paying attention to me! After all, I WAS SELLING TEN DOLLAR BILLS FOR JUST ONE DOLLAR! I had lost him for the second time and I was frustrated because I had been working with him for a year. What added to this frustration was that I KNEW he would love me for what I could do for him! How could he not want to pay attention to what I had to say?

I actually stopped the presentation and pleaded with him to tell me what I was doing wrong. He said nothing was wrong. He then stated that he had to be honest with me; he didn't have a budget to buy anything so he was just meeting with me to be nice. (Why do clients think that wasting our time and disrespecting us as professionals is being nice?)

At that moment, I knew I had to approach things very differently for him to digest how I could rock his world with my service. He told me that he was sorry that he wasted my time. I thanked him for his honesty and I left but I didn't stop thinking about what he said and what I did NOT say.

One of my personal mottos was "No" means "Try Harder." So I accepted the fact that I was accountable for this failure because I was doing something ineffective and I needed to try harder, or in this case try something different.

I was convinced that my presentation just wasn't keeping his attention. I thought of all the things that I should have said to him while I was there. My software didn't need a budget because the return on investment was extremely high and it was fast.

How could I go back to him and deliver this message differently? How could I get him to listen to me? A third presentation was out of the question.

I don't know how I came up with this idea. I don't think I am that smart so it must have been some type of divine intervention. I took my slide deck and for the first time, I really dissected what each bullet said. Why wasn't this working? It was the same deck I used to sell everybody else so why didn't this guy get excited too?

I tried to put myself in his shoes and read my presentation through his eyes. I never really looked at my messaging through my clients' eyes. I always viewed my presentation as MY story and MY COMPANY's story.

I suddenly realized that my client has his own story and his own problems. He didn't care about my company story! I also noticed for the first time that each bullet sounded so generic. I sounded like each of my competitors. I sounded like I could have been selling anything.

I then reviewed our other marketing tools such as brochures, web pages, advertisements, infographics, and anything else I could find that explained what we did for our clients. For the first time, I found myself looking for RESULTS and I realized that they were extremely difficult to find in our current "sales tools!"

I reworded each marketing point. Instead of approaching the communication with "this is what WE can do for you," I changed the wording to be a statement that HE would make.

When I first created these statements, I called them "Challenge Statements." However, when I started to document my experiences, I researched that term. I discovered that the definitions and descriptions were an established legal term. This did not align with what I was doing. I worried that referring to these phrases as Challenge Statements would cause too much confusion.

So I changed the term to "Diagnostic Statements" but quickly discovered this was also an established term used in nursing.

It is because of these past name changes that, "Visualization Diagnostic Statements" has been trademarked. While this current term better describes the science behind what is accomplished, unfortunately, it was a mouthful and difficult to say. Therefore, by combining Visualization and Diagnostics, the word, Visnostics was born and trademarked!

I am explaining this because in a few pages, you will see a copy of the original document. I want to avoid any confusion the different terms may cause the readers. Challenge Statements, Visnostic Statements, Diagnostic Statements, Visualization Diagnostic Statements, and VDS are the same thing. Both the name and the process have evolved throughout the years.

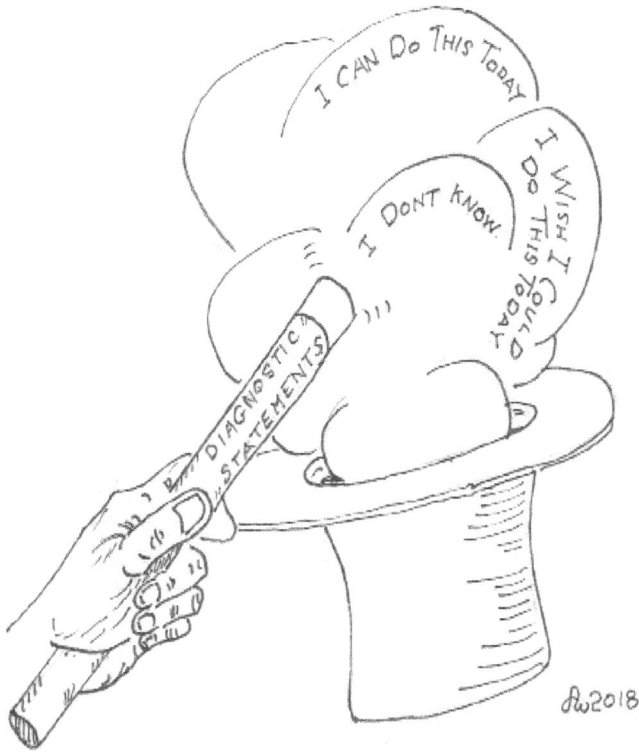

I then made four columns in a Word document. I labeled these columns "Would like to say this," "Say this today," "NA, Not important, or do not know" and "Challenge Statement."

Next, I took each presentation bullet describing the features/functions/benefits of what I was selling and made each bullet a line item. But first I translated them from "We can do this..." into "I can do this..." These became the first "Challenge Statements."

Once this new document was completed, I called the client back and asked him to go to lunch with me. At first, he resisted and reminded me that he didn't have a budget and wasn't going to buy from me. I reassured him that I heard that message loud and clear in our meeting, but I really needed a favor. I promised not to try selling him anything. I just needed his advice on how I could do things better in the future.

I explained that I had created a new tool that I wanted to share and listen to his valuable feedback. Once he knew I wasn't trying to sell him, he agreed to lunch. I suspect there may even be a chapter in neuroscience about our eagerness to respond when someone needs our help.

I could actually feel his defensive walls come crashing down. I'm not sure if it was the offer of a free lunch, the promise that I wasn't going to try and sell him again, or that I needed his help that got me that third meeting. But I do know that his "Fight or Flight" instinct had been disengaged and this was a huge step in correcting what had gone wrong during the first two meetings.

Once we were at lunch and had our food, I pushed my plate aside. I apologized to him for trying to force a presentation. I explained that this time I had a different approach that didn't require a projector, conference room, or even a laptop.

Two Way Communication

All I had was a piece of paper with printing on one side. I told him that I was going to make a statement and with each statement, I would need him to respond with one of three responses. "I can do this today," "I wish I could do this today," or "I don't know, not important, not applicable."

NOTE: After reading this book, Bosworth began referring to these client responses as "AFFIRMATIONS" and he actually wrote about these affirmations in the Foreword. However, be careful not to confuse the client affirmations with the actual statements. A statement is always a statement even after the client responds, but not all client responses will be affirmations. For example, if a client responds to the statement, "not important" or "not applicable," the client response is NOT an affirmation. However, the statement is still a statement. This is an important principle to understand while reading this book.

He agreed and I started with the first line. "Restore is a simple and visual process." His eyes immediately looked up and to the left; I was stunned. I had been taught that salespeople should look for this body language because it meant that the audience was envisioning something that would get them emotionally engaged in the conversation.

To my surprise, not only did he say he WISHED he could do that today, he elaborated on how they did it today and how long it took and how painful it was. He even told me a story about how the CEO had accidentally deleted an email. The CEO frantically called the IT department and explained that this was an emergency and he needed them to restore that email immediately.

However, it took over twenty-four hours to find the backup of the deleted email and restore it. In fact, someone had actually been terminated because it took so long to restore. He explained that the inability of the IT Department to restore lost data in a timely manner was now extremely visible at the CEO level and the IT department was now considered to be incompetent at the highest level within the company.

Wow! That was some valuable information about the "pain" he was feeling in his current role.

I restored the original document I designed in 2004 so I could include a copy to share here. I did edit it and took out all references to what company this was, the competitors, and specific shared applications names that were needed.

Don't bother trying to read it. I just want you to see how unpolished it was.

Despite being primitive, ugly, and very simplistic, it was so much more effective than my gorgeous, fifty slides, professionally crafted presentation that the company provided to me! How crazy is THAT?!

Company Name:
Date: 2004
Because the XYZ solution is very robust, and we have a limited amount of time to demonstrate the software, please take a moment to answer the following questions so our presentation can be customized for you and your company.

1. Attendees

Name	Title	Function

2. Specific "Deleted" Concerns – What are THREE "challenges" that you are tasked with or most concerned about?

Name	Challenge #1	Challenge #2	Challenge #3
	Compliancy	No budget	With (competitors name) today

3. Please put a check mark next to one of the three options describing your current situation with back-up and restore

Would LIKE to say this	SAY this TODAY	NA, Not Important or do not know (?)	Challenge Statement
✓			Restore is a simple and visual process
	✓		Quickly and easily find and restore missing files
✓			Avoid wasteful and costly differential back-up jobs
✓			In seconds, scroll back in time to view past server state
✓			Missing files and directories are seen as conspicuous cross-hatched objects and a single click launches the restore job
✓			Reduce hardware costs by exploiting inexpensive serial ATA-devices.
	✓		Decrease backup time
✓			Ultra quick restores from disk
✓			Integrate Disk-to-Disk-to-Tape with Synthetic Full Backup to maximize benefits.
		N/A	Backup time shrinks drastically
✓			Only incremental backups are needed. (XYZ performs full back-ups1x wk)
✓			Reduce network traffic by only sending incremental data over the LAN.
✓			Restore time is optimized since restore is from the synthetic full job on disk/tape.
✓			Potentially run incremental backups forever and synthetic fulls.
✓			Avoid wasteful and costly differential back-up jobs
	✓		Create offsite tapes during your regular, nightly backups
✓			Simultaneously write to disk and tape
✓			Save time by not having to re-run backups or having to duplicate tapes during the day.
✓			The ability to backup through a single port created as a secure outbound connection.
✓			No open (inbound) ports are needed for backup
	✓		The ability to restart a job from the point of failure
		?	The ability to pause an active job midstream?
		?	Failed backup jobs over the LAN can be automatically restarted and pick-up from where they left off and not restart the job over from the beginning
	✓		Pause and restart an active job at any time for any reason
		?	Ability to restore your own data through a web browser
		?	Personalize XML-based reports
✓			Align costs with SLAs
✓			Vendor appreciates you and treats you as a valued partner

I know it's impossible to read. I was selling business continuity software. However, no need to spend any time trying to read the details in the "Statement" section because the details are not important. Just know that each statement started out as a bullet in a presentation; this was the same presentation during which this client fell asleep and wrote his grocery list! And yet his reaction to this approach was completely opposite of my professional presentation. Nobody was more surprised than me at this stage of my career!

The reality is that the client doesn't care about all the cosmetics if you can't get him/her engaged in the content and have an intelligent, two-way dialogue.

If the client isn't talking, the salesperson isn't learning how to help the client!

I realize that this sounds so logical and simple. However, all sales professionals know just how difficult it can be to get clients to share information. And now we know WHY – "The Fight or Flight" instinct is a powerful adversary during each sales cycle.

The secret to overcoming this response is to get them emotionally, not just intellectually, engaged.

Creating effective Visnostic Statements and asking your audience to reflect and respond is the tactical instruction that has been missing from every sales methodology book that I have read.

This Visnostic process is unique and like nothing you have ever been taught until now.

It's important to understand that this isn't a theory or hypothesis. It is a methodology that I have been utilizing for over ten years and it has worked at multiple companies with different products and services.

It is also an approach that none of my clients have ever seen another salesperson do. It is a universal technique and since nobody is doing it, it will be refreshing to your clients when you approach them with this new communication style. That is until the lessons taught in this book become normal business practices.

This process has evolved but I will help you with the basics first and then I will explain some enhancements that have been added through the years. And as I demonstrated earlier, it doesn't have to be pretty to be effective.

About half-way through the list of my Visnostic Statements, he pushed his plate of food aside and he commented that he assumed my company could do all this or we wouldn't be going through this exercise. I said that was correct. He then asked me why the heck I didn't tell him this before now!

I looked him straight in the eyes and told him that this is the presentation that I gave him TWICE! **He laughed and said none of it even sounded familiar to him.**

This is when I realized that marketing content relies too heavily on clients' abilities to translate and interpret the actual benefits.

This new way of presenting the same information was allowing me to guide him through the thought process by eliminating the translation requirement. The result was that instead of dumping everything I could do for my client in a presentation and depending on him to translate, I was able to guide him to his own conclusion.

I also noticed that I talked a lot less and the client talked a lot more. In fact, I noticed how passionately the client started opening up to me! This was an incredible thing to witness! I NEVER got this type of reaction during a presentation!

The client came to his own conclusion versus me telling him what to think. When it is his or her idea, they will become more receptive.

He then asked if I could send him an electronic version of this new document, including his responses, by close of business that same day! I said of course!

I left the meeting and typed it all up, along with some of his commentary, which I had written on the back of this paper. He called me the next day with questions. He confessed that he edited the document and was presenting it to the CEO as his own research with a recommendation to go with us to fix specific problems that would address the restoration delays the CEO had witnessed.

Within a month of this lunch, the deal closed and it made my number for the entire year. This was a client that had no budget and obviously no interest in my presentation because **his mind was on his own problems, not what my company had to say about our company.** Aren't most clients having this same experience when we take their valuable time?

Salespeople talk way too much about their company and what they can do. Companies need their marketing departments to address this immediately! I can honestly say that nobody has ever bought from me because of the stock prices, our acquisitions, or the company strategy. They buy because of the positive way their business will be impacted. I hope as people from both sales and marketing read the Visnostic books, they see their messaging from a completely different perspective so it can be changed!

How can you fix something that you didn't realize was broken?

My content was exactly the same. The only difference was the way in which the content was communicated.

This was when I realized that HOW you articulate your message is more important than the actual content!

I felt like I had just invented the light bulb with this new approach! "No" means "Try Harder" or in this case, "No" meant that I needed to try something different.

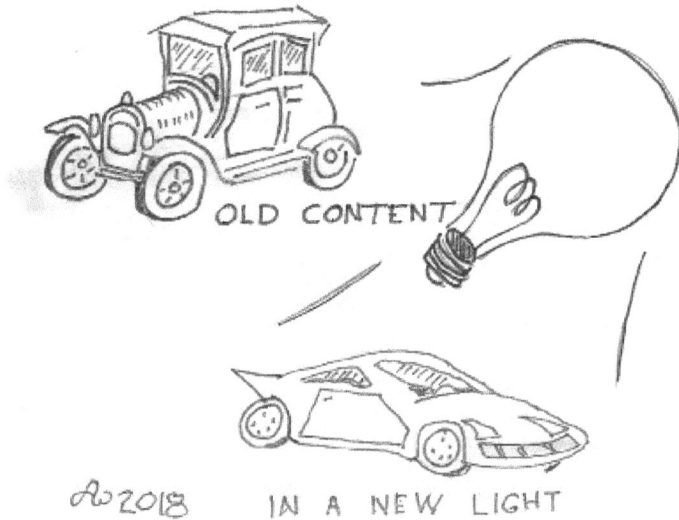

OLD CONTENT

Ao 2018   IN A NEW LIGHT

This story happened over 10 years ago and I have successfully used this approach at both big companies and small companies. I was never sure why this worked or what to call it. But as I read Mike Bosworth's most recent book, *What Great Salespeople Do*, I finally understood that this wasn't just dumb luck; there is some heavy-duty science behind it. Today, we call it Neuroscience. And it's powerful because it works!

Since 2004, I have been converting presentation bullets into this format and taking this approach with my clients with huge success. This methodology has even evolved into something more powerful. Today, when a client responds with "I can do or say this today," I now ask him to grade himself with a one through five rating system.

The scoring goes like this; if the client gives himself a one, that means they can do it but they have a lot of room for improvement. If the client scores himself a five, it means that he can do it today and he views it as perfect.

Now that you know the history of Visualization Diagnostic Statements as well as some of its evolution over the past decade, let's review some basic neuroscience that you will soon observe first hand. I am confident that each reader will be amazed to find this part of the book to be enlightening and fun.

Fun facts about how your brain works

3 CANDLES

3 MICE

3 PEAKS

AJ 2018

The Power of THREEs

You are about to have your first experience with executing neuroscience exercises. Some of the exercises will go extremely well while others will have some challenges and may not even work at all. But don't be discouraged.

Activities before and during the learning process will increase your retention of the content. After you read the entire book, go back and retry the exercises to see how much you have improved. It will be a great opportunity to see your progress while you evaluate your understanding of this new approach. It will also build your confidence that you are ready to execute with your clients.

There are so many books out today about neuroscience, which is basically a cool new buzzword for psychology. One of the points I read recently about neuroscience is to engage with your clients as soon as possible, which is why chapter one starts with some executable exercises for the reader.

I also attended a leadership conference for women recently that taught the audience that the male brain prefers to have selections in groups of threes. To prove her point, the speaker showed us advertisements for three different tires. The speaker also told us that men prefer three colors of pants in their wardrobe: black, khaki, and blue. She supported these claims by having the only six men in the audience come on stage and she was correct; they all had on those colors of pants. These two simple new things I learned, helped validate why what I am about to share with you really does work and it works well!

The purpose of this story is to help you understand why I have three exercises for you to do in Chapter One, why you will see other topics in this book developed in sets of three.

And more importantly – **Why Visnostic Statements Have THREE Options For Your Clients To Consider!**

Per the facts mentioned above, at least fifty percent of our population prefers choices in threes or odd numbers. But I actually think the percentage is much higher.

3 CANDLES

The points made about men's brains reminded me of a woman's decorating class that taught that we think we want symmetrical settings, but our brain actually prefers things in uneven numbers.

Therefore, it can be concluded that these preferences in groups of threes may apply to women as well as men.

As you conduct Visnostic discussion, you will be tempted to take short cuts or simplify by just offering ONE of the THREE selections but if you do that, you just converted a statement into a question! AND you will be eliminating the POWER OF THREES! Do NOT do that!

You will make your Visnostic STATEMENT (speaking from the Client's perspective) and ask them to select one of three responses:

1. **I can say this today. (If so, score yourself 1-5 with 5 being perfect)**
2. **I WISH I could say this today.**
3. **It's not important, I don't know, or not applicable.**

Visnostic Discussions are NOT Questions!
Questions are risky and can trigger the "Fight or Flight" instinct that we all have.

People that sell training on how to ask questions will argue this claim so let me give an example to prove my point – Do you get excited and eager when you receive a call from someone asking you to spend just a few minutes as they conduct a survey? Do you eagerly wait after a support call so you can respond to the survey about your satisfaction with the call? If you answer yes, you are an anomaly. For most people, this is an annoyance. We need to know what is in it for US? If you write your statements correctly, your first three words will clearly explain what is in it for your audience.

For more information, please look in the Appendix; you will find additional articles that will support the points I make about Visnostic Statements and why statements are much more impactful than questions. But the reality is that we will never eliminate the need for SOME questions as we interact with others.

Fight or Flight or Freeze

There are a few fundamental human instincts to keep in mind as you read the following directions. First of all, "fight or flight" is a real thing that haunts salespeople. Humans have a natural instinct to put up walls, become defensive, or flee when someone is trying to sell to them, ask them for money, or persuade them.

You don't believe this? When you see a sales call on your caller ID, do you enthusiastically answer your phone? When you answer the phone and it is a charity or salesperson, do you hang-up on them? Do you interrupt and tell them that you don't have time to talk? What other tactics do you use to avoid listening to them pitch to you? When you walk into a store, and a salesperson asks if they can help you, do you attempt to brush them off by telling them that you are just looking? Your responses were probably very much like the responses you have towards SURVEYS (i.e. QUESTIONS)!

As you read that there will be exercises, do you recall how that made you feel? Even if it occurred in your subconscious, I bet that you already decided and JUSTIFIED why you don't need to do the exercises. Am I right? Humans are complex but we can be incredibly predictable as well.

Because I have been selling my entire career, you would think that I would be more receptive and patient with salespeople. However, I am far from it. I even took the time to add all of my numbers to the United States Do Not Call Registry.

The **Do Not Call Registry** accepts registrations from both cell phones and land lines. To **register** by telephone, **call** 1-888-382-1222 (TTY: 1-866-290-4236). You must **call** from the phone number that you want to **register**. To **register** online (**donotcall**.gov), you **will** have to respond to a confirmation email.

Sadly, it hasn't helped at all. Salespeople are annoying because our brains are wired to flee from persuasive scenarios. Those that force us to do things that are unnatural are difficult to trust.

Visnostics is how to sell without getting the negative reaction that naturally occurs towards sales efforts.

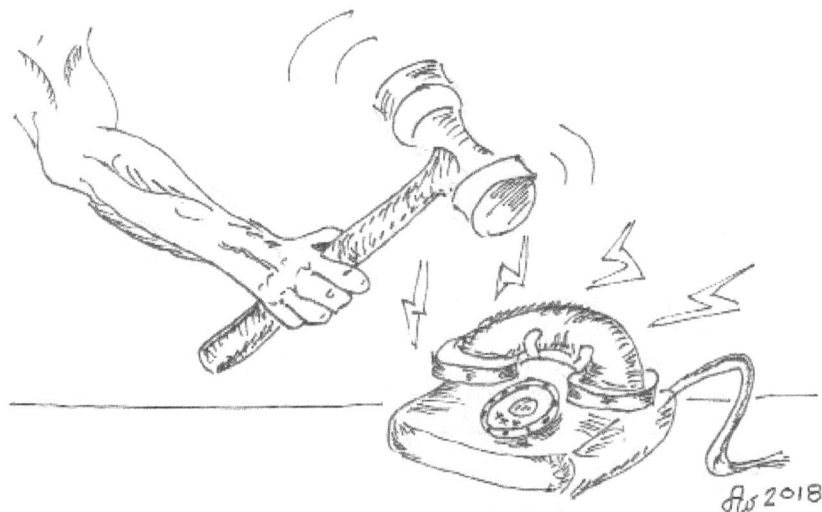

Do Not Call

With the "Fight or Flight" instinct in mind, it is important that these exercises are not conducted without an explanation that will ensure that your participant's defensive walls are down. Please inform your participant that you are doing an experiment from a book you are reading. Then ask if they would please help you by participating by responding to a few statements.

Remember that most people enjoy an opportunity to help as long as there isn't a catch or a hidden agenda.

Fight your Flight instincts and do these exercises!

The Power of Visualization

What does Visualization mean to you? Visualization is often described using several words like conversion, translation, interpretation, and envisioning. What if your vision is different than what your client is envisioning? Translating is hard work as well as risky because it can lead to misinterpretation. It is the biggest reason for lost sales and even lost clients.

Words such as "considerable," "extensive," "immediate," or "quickly" are subjective and can cause miscommunication between you and your client. You could be setting yourself up for a future dissatisfied client. In addition, slang, acronyms and industry jargon are dangerous. **Visnostics will help you translate!**

A Different Type of Christmas Story

I want to share a story of a deal I lost due to two different visions of what my company could do for a client.

There was a time when companies needed to migrate data from one device to another device. To do this, companies had to bring down production to do a migration and holidays were a common time to do this due to low activity. I sold software that allowed companies to do this migration while production was live. Needless to say, this was a pretty easy sale.

I was in Dallas at a major retailer's headquarters and I had already done a lot of homework. One of the men was a technical influencer and he mentioned to me that he hadn't been home with his family on Christmas Day in years. He explained that he would watch his children open their gifts and then head to the office for the rest of the day. I couldn't wait to give him the good news! He would never miss Christmas with his family ever again!

I thought I nailed the presentation! So you can imagine my shock at how quickly I was told that I would not be winning their business. I went back to their office to find out what I did wrong. To my surprise, the man that told me about working Christmas Day admitted that he killed the deal.

His reason was very simple. He relied very heavily on the triple pay he got on Christmas Day to buy the gifts for his family each year. Therefore, he viewed our services as a threat, not a benefit. When he told me that he hadn't been home in years, I interpreted that as a bad thing. I found out too late that he actually depended on it and there were other days he got extra pay that my company and I would eliminate. In other words, my offering hurt him and his family personally! This was a very painful lesson about the risk involved when translating sales benefits to client benefits. I would have bet my commission check that he viewed me as his HEROINE, not his VILLAIN!

A great Visnostic Statement for this would have been, "I will never have to work on weekends or holidays ever again!" His reply would have been "Not important, not applicable, or I don't know" which would have been a huge indicator for me to get clarification from the client BEFORE I went in with guns-a-blazing about how he would get to spend Christmas with his family!

There are at least two types of translations that take place during a sales cycle. Salespeople are trying to map their products and services to the pain and need of the client and the client is trying to interpret how the features and functions of the vendor's offering will convert to his or her world. This is a universal issue and yet we continue to handle it poorly.

We need to take the translation risks out of the sales cycle.

Visualization Diagnostic Statements will flush out these important facts before you ever even present to your client!

EXERCISE #1
The Power of Visualization

This is very simple to do and it works every single time!

In 2007, I was part of a transformation team that toured the country teaching "Order Takers" how to be "Hunters." I began my presentation with a little exercise that I want you to try before you read any further.

I don't know where you are right now. You may be on a plane, or reading this in bed before you go to sleep, or on a lunch break. It doesn't matter where you are right now; what matters is that you have an innocent bystander that you can nab and ask him or her to participate in an exercise that will take less than 15 seconds.

If you are alone, DO NOT be tempted to pick up the phone to call someone because it is important that you watch the participant's eyes. After you explain this is an experiment, just say these simple words –

"I am going to say a word and I need you to tell me the first VISUAL that pops into your head. What is the first thing you SEE when you hear this word...."

(Pause) Are you ready? (Pause)
"MONEY"

Be sure to carefully watch the eyes.

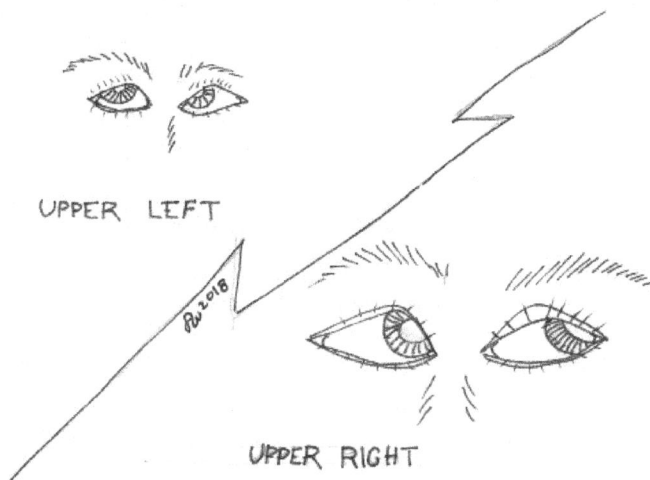

UPPER LEFT

UPPER RIGHT

The eyes will move rather fast so if you blink, you may miss it. Often, you will see them look up to the right or up to the left. As sales professionals, we should know the basics of body language and this means they are thinking and visualizing something.

Ask them to be as detailed as possible when describing what they see. It's incredible how fast our minds visualize memories. Please send me an email describing what they say to you to this email address – **money@dynaexec.com**.

 It is important that you follow these instructions because emailing me a description of what happened will help reinforce what you saw and learned. Those that skip this step will not improve as much as those that take time to reflect, envision, and document the observations of this exercise.

Lessons Learned From Exercise #1

There are so many lessons to be learned by doing this exercise.

One lesson is that our minds visualize things extremely fast when it is something to which we can relate.

Another lesson is that different minds process data differently. For example, I often get short answers during this exercise but every once in awhile; a person will describe what sounds like a movie! Sometimes when I ask what a person visualizes, instead, they describe FEELINGS.

I was with a lady that I have hired three different times. She is the best salesperson and relationship builder I have ever met. However, I consistently had challenges keeping her focused. I always assumed it was because she has been diagnosed with ADD.

As we reviewed the draft of this book together, I became very aware that her brain moves faster and with many more details than other people. What she described to me when she heard the word "Money" was extremely emotional and thorough. She described money as being a source of freedom and then gave me multiple examples. The word triggered more emotions from her than any other person I have ever encountered. Her explanation went on for over ten minutes and her eyes were darting in every direction.

I realized that not only did I get an understanding of how she views the word "money,' I also got an education on how different her thought process is compared to other people that have done this exercise with me. I was seeing firsthand how difficult it is for a person with such an active brain to be focused on one thing at a time.

I realized that I needed to be aware of how her brain processes information and visualizes conversations so I can understand how I might want to adjust my own communication style with her. This will be enlightening as you get to know new clients as well. As she was talking, I wondered how many brains like hers have been diagnosed as having ADD when in reality their brains are much more active than other brains. To me, what I was witnessing was a gift or talent versus a handicap or disability as ADD is often viewed.

A few weeks later, I did this same exercise with a relative and she said she has so many negative feelings around the word money. She also went into great detail about the bad feelings that surfaced when she heard this word.

Words can trigger unexpected emotional responses.

Both of these ladies described **feelings** when they heard the word versus an **image**. One responded positively emotionally and the other responded negatively. The word was the same but the responses and perceptions were complete opposites. Why does this matter? Those of you that watched the video I recommended in the Introduction will know exactly why this is important to understand.

If you are presenting, you are assuming that your audience comprehends your message the way you intend it to be received. But how can you determine if you are accomplishing this goal? How do you determine how your client is processing information? Those that visualize a movie may have a more challenging time keeping up during a fast-paced presentation. This reaction may cause you to lose important points with some members of your audience.

What if I told you that Visnostic Statements will ensure that your clients communicate their interpretation of your messaging? This will enable you to avoid miscommunication from occurring.

Getting your audience to visualize and articulate their current situation is the most impactful way to get them emotionally engaged in your conversation. Their comments will also validate their comprehension of the points you are making.

During this exercise, the more details your participant gives you, the more emotional engagement you will observe. The eyes will reveal additional emotions and you can observe the magnitude of the visualizations taking place in their mind.

Now let's discuss why most people will resist following the instructions around this exercise.

While writing and sharing with a test group, not one person followed the instructions or shared their experience with me via email as requested. This in itself is proof that when someone feels they are being coerced or persuaded to do something, the natural instinct is to rebel and flee. It was simply too much work for the reader. So why do we expect a different response from our clients? Translating is hard work. That makes it very risky for sales because it can lead to misinterpretations by your clients.

The more work you do for the client, the more you will be perceived as adding value and the more receptive your client will be to your message.

fw 2018

I did this exercise with one of my favorite recruiters and she told me that she saw an orange. Because that was the first time I had ever heard that response, I asked her to elaborate on why she saw an orange. She explained that money buys her food and she loves oranges. So this conversation with my recruiter is even more evidence of how one single word can mean so many different things to many different people. As salespeople, one of our biggest challenges is to understand how our audience is interpreting our words.

Words translate differently because we each have different experiences. One single word can mean different things triggering completely different emotions within each person.

I recall many conversations I have had with clients over the years where we had communication challenges. Often, their interpretations of industry terms such as "the cloud" or "implementation" were very different than my company or mine.

When I wrote my first book, I decided I wanted to leverage a Publisher. I learned quickly that my vision of the role a Publisher would play in my life was very different than the vision my Publisher had. This different expectation of what a Publisher is has caused a great deal of disappointment for both of us.

I'm sure you can think of a communication breakdown you've had recently due to different interpretations of what words meant. In fact, any married person should have LOTS of stories!

As I described in an earlier story, even working on Christmas Day can have different perspectives and produce different emotional responses. Understanding your client's unique visualizations will help you exceed versus falling short of their expectations. You have probably heard that studies show most sales are lost due to a communication failure. Personally, I think this simplifies why most sales are lost but this communication breakdown is why this book is so important.

Wouldn't it be cool if you could get into your clients' heads? Once you are aware of their visualizations, you won't make the mistake of focusing on YOUR visions by accident as I did in my previous Christmas Day Story.

Diagnostic Statements flush out your clients' visualizations thus reducing the risk of communication misinterpretations, disappointments, disconnects, or breakdowns.

Too many times, the client's expectations do not match the salesperson's interpretations of those expectations.

These communication challenges often result in unnecessary lost sales. But this can be avoided with some simple changes to how we communicate.

I have conducted the "money" exercise hundreds of times since 2007. Most people say they see physical items such as bags of money, coins, stacks of currency, and bags of gold. Others see symbols like a $ dollar, € Euro, ¥ Yen, or £ Pound. Some of the more creative and humorous responses I have heard are things like the alimony check I write each month, my mortgage payment, bills, my tuition payment, my home, my children, my spouse, my parents...the list goes on and on.

The main lesson learned in Exercise #1 may shock many readers but **there are no right or wrong answers when asked to describe what is visualized when hearing the word *MONEY*. This exercise** demonstrated that each person will TRANSLATE or convert those letters into something meaningful that is unique to him or her.

Therefore, this exercise proves that presenting WHAT your company does and WHY it does it, is NOT effective and is high risk. Your client's may not translate your words as you intended!

The biggest surprise in this exercise is not what people say in response. It is what they DON'T say that should make every single reader change the way in which he or she communicates.

Here is the part of Exercise #1 that should make those light bulbs start going off for many readers:

Despite receiving hundreds of different responses, not one single person has EVER said they saw a slide with a bullet and the LETTERS

M

O

N

E

Y

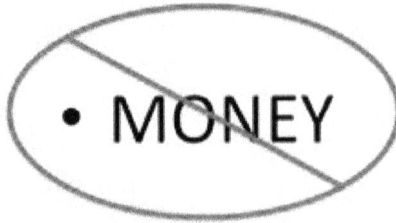

We simply do not visualize letters or words. In fact, our brains are a lot like a computer. Computers convert 1's and 0's to something on the screen that we can comprehend.

EXERCISE #2
The Power of Translation

Below is a sentence written with binary code. You can search for "binary code translator" and type these numbers into it and it will automatically translate it for you.

Less than 1% of you will be curious enough to figure out how to translate it. That means 99% of you will engage your flight instinct to justify avoiding that effort.

**01010000 01100101 01101111 01110000 01101100
01100101 00100000 01100001 01110110 01101111
01101001 01100100 00100000 01110100 01110010
01100001 01101110 01110011 01101100 01100001
01110100 01101001 01101111 01101110 00100001**

Our brains do the same thing when they convert letters to physical things that we can comprehend. Just as computers translate zeros and ones into letters and symbols, salespeople need to translate letters and words into visualization for our clients!

So my questions to each reader are:

WHY DO WE KEEP PRESENTING SLIDES LOADED WITH BULLETS AND LETTERS?

WHY DO WEBSITES HAVE MORE WORDS THAN GRAPHICS?

WHY DO THE GRAPHICS NOT EVEN MATCH THE MESSAGE?

WHY ARE MOST BUSINESS BOOKS FULL OF WORDS YET VERY FEW PICTURES?

WHY CREATE ANY MARKETING MATERIALS LOADED WITH PICTURES THAT HAVE ZERO TO DO WITH THE TOPIC?

Your communication, presentations, websites, and advertisements MUST have visuals and these visuals must tie back to your message...

...But only if you want your audience to Relate (understand), Retain (remember), and Repeat (give you referrals)

Does your message tell a story that helps ensure your client can Relate, Retain, and Repeat?

These are the Three R's of Visualization
Diagnostic Statements
Relate - Retain – Repeat

With the "Three R's" in mind, let's stop for a moment and reflect on the first story in this book. Remember the roast story with the mother and daughter? As you read this, what did you visualize? Do you see the drawings or do you see the letters in the story?

What about the Christmas Story? Do you "see" the wreath? Do you remember the story?

What about the graphic with the little guy that had on boxing gloves and then another graphic of him running? What did that graphic represent?

You REMEMBER those stories, don't you? Neuroscience is so predictable and so universally effective. Why aren't we leveraging it in our communications with EVERYBODY?

I ask you again, "Why do our marketing materials, slides, brochures, websites, and infographics have so many words?" Why do we prefer to watch videos on YouTube instead of reading how to do something?

The answer is that we want that visual translation done for us. We don't want our brains to do that work. We are only human. And guess what? The last time I checked, our clients are human too.

Ideally, marketing will create Visnostic messaging. However, if they don't, it is up to the salesperson to convert and translate those features and functions into something that the client can relate to, comprehend, understand, and VISUALIZE.

And guess what? When a salesperson is forced to do this, they aren't selling. Relying on sales to do this is a costly decision but it's the only way I've been able to convert features and functions into meaningful Visnostic content that my clients are craving.

This hasn't been marketing's fault; Visnostics aren't taught in college (YET) and most marketing teams won't learn Visnostics in a traditional marketing role. For marketing departments to stop the madness that is product marketing, they will have to change the way in which they operate.

When was the last time your marketing team interacted with your existing client base? How does marketing create case studies or track ROI (Return on Investments) with clients? As marketing departments become more interactive with clients, they may uncover unique ways clients benefit that are excluded in the current messaging. This has happened to me multiple times in my career!

The most common mistake I see sales and companies make is to list out all their features and functions with the expectation that the clients will accurately TRANSLATE those details into how it applies to their own world. Depending upon clients to make that translation is a huge mistake. It is extremely risky to assume your clients WANT to convert your presentation or if they even know how!

And one of the guiltiest professions around is REAL ESTATE! Do you ever take clients to a house and just stand there and expect THEM to visualize how they would live in that house? Sorry to offend you but that is the laziest form of selling that there is. In fact, that isn't selling, that is ORDER TAKING.

The good news is that this is one of the easiest professions to fix, which is why this special edition was written. Chapter 2 is customized 100% for Real Estate Agents.

Have you ever watched HGTV? My husband and I love *Bargain Beach Hunt* and it's become a joke between us when the Buyers tell the Agent that they want two bedrooms and two bathrooms. We usually laugh and joke that they will end up with a one bedroom or efficiency on the beach! And it's a little shocking how often we are correct! So as you read the next chapter, try and reflect on how many people you have talked with that told you what they thought they wanted yet bought something completely different. It's not the Buyers fault when this happens; **it's actually the Agent's responsibility to help them VISUALIZE how they will truly live in the property.** How they live is often very different than what they THINK they want. If you talk with top Agents, I'm confident they will agree that they try upfront to really understand their Buyer's VISION.

The best Real Estate Agents MATCH DREAMS to the right PROPERTIES instead of selling houses with bedrooms and bathrooms to Buyers.

I can't wait to read the emails and messages about how these simple changes will positively impact your business!

I know you will enjoy the rest of the book!

CHAPTER TWO –

Special Edition - Visnostics for Agents

As you can imagine, I have been talking about these principles to many people with various careers. I had a Real Estate Agent friend of mine say that this doesn't apply to their business because clients buy homes based upon the number of bedrooms and bathrooms. I thought that was an interesting perspective. The best Real Estate Agent I ever met told me that she didn't sell homes she sold dreams. She sold us two homes and not once did we discuss the number of bedrooms or bathrooms. Instead, she asked me to describe how I envisioned living in my next home.

I explained that our friends lost all of their children in a fire because all the kids were upstairs and the master was downstairs. I told her I would like the downstairs to have a nice flow for entertaining but that I preferred all the bedrooms be located upstairs. I described wanting to wake up in the mornings and step out on the balcony that overlooked a pool. I wanted fireplaces downstairs but I thought a fireplace in the master bedroom was romantic. I told her that I didn't care about the kitchen because I prefer to eat out but that I wanted a breakfast area to drink coffee and look at the pool. I explained that my husband and I both needed offices away from each other. I told her that I loved the look of a spiraling staircase but that wasn't mandatory. As I described these things to her, I felt emotional and anxious while I wondered if my perfect dream home even existed.

Well, it did exist. It was the first and only house she showed us and it was nothing like we imagined. It was a Georgian Style and that wasn't something we thought we wanted. When we pulled up, my husband didn't even want to go inside. But the Agent talked us into taking a look because she said she thought we would be surprised. As we walked through the house, my husband was unimpressed with the colors and the style. But I realized she was showing me my exact description! She did a great job bringing my thoughts to the surface so as I walked through the house, those thoughts were already on my mind and I was able to help my husband see the home's potential. I instantly imagined how we would live in the house. I never even noticed how many bedrooms. For the record, it had five but two of them became offices. We bought this house in 2000 and have lived in our dream home ever since.

Do you realize all the time and inconvenience this agent managed to avoid for **all** concerned? She was brilliant for asking me to describe how I wanted to **live in the house** instead of asking how many bedrooms or bathrooms we **THOUGHT** we wanted. This quick sell gave her more time to show more homes to more people. If we ever sell, she will be the first one I call because I know there won't be a lot of unnecessary strangers in our home.

I see Real Estate ads all the time that describe the number of bedrooms and the number of bathrooms along with a picture of a home and the square footage.

If we had seen an elevation of our current home with a description of five bedrooms and four bathrooms, we would have never agreed to look at it!

So do ads that start off with the number of bedrooms and bathrooms really do an effective job attracting the right buyers to the right homes?

Our Agent did us a great service by asking how we envisioned living in the home versus asking us what features and functions we THOUGHT we wanted. By doing this, she triggered emotions that I didn't even know I had! She was using neuroscience before I even knew what it was!

3 BEDROOM, 2 BATH HOME AND 30X40 SHOP FOR SALE IN
WASHINGTON SCHOOL DISTRICT ON 2.4 ACRES

POSTED ON MAY 28, 2019 BY DEBORAH

Sweet little home that's neat as a pen, on rural acreage with no restrictions! 2.4 acres is fenced on all 3 sides... has a nice 30X40 metal shop with RV hookup, concrete floor, has electric and plumbed for water and sewer. Good production water well and City Water Tap is installed, but not in use. All this in the Washington School District! What are you waiting for!

Is this what your home ads look like? What if someone just needs one bedroom but two offices? Are the bedrooms, bathrooms, and square footage descriptions you share forcing your potential clients to TRANSLATE how they would use it?

The advertisement above says this house is in the Washington School District. Is that a good thing? Your potential client may need to go do research to find out why that is important. And since we just learned in Chapter One that people avoid making that extra effort, will they ignore the ad and keep looking? Did the author of this listing assume all potential buyers would automatically know that Washington School District is a selling point?

Now read the description again; it says "rural acreage with no restrictions." Why is that important? Is it because there are no HOA dues? But does it also mean that my neighbors can have a pig farm next door? Again, each person is going to translate that into something that they can relate to and **it won't always be a good thing.** This form of advertising is dangerous because you have no idea if your audience is interpreting your points as a positive or negative attribute of the home!

EXERCISE #3
The Power of Translation (continued)

I challenge you to rewrite the captions on the home ad on page 90 using a Visnostic style to guide your reader to a positive conclusion.

Since I originally shared this story in *Visnostic Selling*, I've had numerous workshops with various Real Estate Agencies and I want to share one of my favorite success stories.

There was a very generic house that had been on the market for six months with a real estate agency and it had very few showings and no offerings. Needless to say, when the contract on the original listing expired, the sellers went with another agency and it just happened to be awarded to one of the readers of Visnostic Selling.

This new agent published a "Coming Soon" ad with a photo of the house but instead of stating the usual number of bedrooms and bathrooms, the caption went something like this:

I can walk to the boat ramp and take a relaxing ride on the lake after a long day at the office. I don't have to worry when the kids are playing in the backyard because the swimming pool has a secure safety fence separating it from the fun and colorful playground. And mornings are a breeze with the spacious kitchen that gives us all plenty of room to grab breakfast while lunches are prepared on the huge island. The open floor plan has the perfect place for a Christmas tree yet plenty of room for the entire family to gather and roast marshmallows in the fire-burning fireplace.

This is the perfect dream house for a busy young family to make lasting memories. If you wish you could say this about YOUR home, come to the open house this Saturday...blah blah blah...

When the new listing agent arrived 15 minutes prior to the open house, she was pleasantly surprised to see several people already in line! The house received multiple offers that first day and sold for $30,000 over the asking price!

Remember, this same house was listed with another agent for six months with very few viewings and no offers. The original agent advertised the old-fashioned way by leading with square footage and the number of bedrooms and bathrooms.

But that's not all! The new listing agent signed three more listings because several people that saw the advertisement wanted her to market their homes the same way!

Why do you think you need to talk square footage, number of bedrooms, and number of bathrooms?

Just like the moral in the "Roast Story," don't just do it that way because that's the way everybody else does it. Why not get more scientific and help your potential buyers actually ENJOY the buying experience? You may even enjoy your job more too!

Reader Story – David Stoltzman – Randy White Real Estate Services

I was working with a young man that just started in the real-estate business and he read *Visnostic Selling* and really embraced it. One of the chapters dives deep into what I call "Segmentation." This is when you reflect on your different types of audiences and determine how you can categorize your message to each of their specific priorities.

First of all, how does a Real Estate Agent choose to be with one agency over another? So one of the segmentation groups should be geared towards **recruiting** the best talent to your agency.

Then once you are staffed up, you will want to attract potential **clients that want to sell their homes**. This will build an inventory of homes to sell. And once you have listings, you will want to **appeal to the actual Buyers.**

This young man was new but he is sharp and he pointed out that a fourth segmentation is also needed that would be written for **both Buyers and Sellers**. Here are the Visnostic Statements this future Real Estate Super-Star sent me after reading just the first chapter of *Visnostic Selling*:

SELLERS -

Please choose one of these three responses to each statement below.

- **I can say this today!**
- **I WISH I could say this today!**
  or
- **It's not important, not applicable, or I don't know.**

I know exactly what price my home would sell for today.
I am aware of what I will net at closing when I sell my home.
I already have my next home picked out.
I have a timeline for when I want to sell and be in my next home.
My home is the top-viewed home on Zillow for my neighborhood.
My home is ready to be photographed and is staged appropriately for marketing.
My home could sell for top-dollar in its current condition.
I desire a hands-off, resort-like experience when selling my home.
If I am not satisfied with my Agent's performance + communication, I want the option to cancel our agreement.

What other statements would you say that were omitted?

Write them out here:

BUYERS -

Please choose one of these three responses to each statement below.

- **I can say this today!**
- **I WISH I could say this today!**
  or
- **It's not important, not applicable, or I don't know.**

I know the home buying process in Texas from beginning to end.
My Agent only shows me homes in my criteria, or I request to see.
My Agent doesn't obligate or "hard sell" me on a particular home.
My Agent points out minor and major cosmetic/material flaws in every home we see.
I receive comps on every home I consider offering on, so I don't over-extend.
My Agent has an "off-market" list, and reaches out to other agents for "coming soon" listings.
I'm confident I know what my closing costs will be on buying a home.
I don't feel nervous or anxious about buying a home.
I can effectively forecast appreciation for each home I see.

What other statements would you say that were omitted?

Write them out here:

BUYERS AND SELLERS –

Please choose one of these three responses to each statement below.

- **I can say this today!**
- **I WISH I could say this today!**
  or
- **It's not important, not applicable, or I don't know**

I have a trusted Agent-resource for my neighborhood.
My Agent has an extensive track record selling homes.
I communicate regularly with my current Real Estate-resource.
I have other resources i.e. local lenders, licensed contractors, inspectors, and other top professionals.
I feel comfortable navigating the TREC contract, addendums, amendments, disclosures, title docs and survey.
I can confidently negotiate on my behalf what is important to me in a real estate transaction.
My Agent communicates with us on nights and weekends, if needed.
I know how to interpret a closing disclosure so I know who pays for what in a transaction.
I know the tangible and intangible factors that drive home prices in my area.

What other statements would you say that were omitted?

Write them out here:

And then finally, what if you owned an agency and you wanted to recruit top talent? What types of Visnostic Statements would differentiate your agency from the competition?

<table>
<tr><td></td></tr>
<tr><td></td></tr>
<tr><td></td></tr>
<tr><td></td></tr>
</table>

The Visnostic Statements David created are exceptionally good, especially for someone that has never thought this way or articulated a message by leveraging visualizations. However, two chapters of my books are dedicated to helping you write the absolute best and strongest statements possible.

This special edition is not intended to replace *VISNOSTIC SALES AND MARKETING*. Instead, its purpose is to teach you just enough to make a positive impact on your communications style today. What will separate the Superstars from the other Real Estate Agents will be that hunger to get even better at this new communication style. Those of you with strong ambition will want to advance to the next level by reading *VISNOSTIC SALES AND MARKETING* or contacting DynaExec to setup a workshop for your team.

VISNOSTIC SALES AND MARKETING has two entire chapters dedicated to creating the absolute most powerful Visnostic Statements. But for this shorter version of the book, here is a synopsis –

RTH

I'm actually using an acronym here to prove a point. Do you realize how overused acronyms are today? From a Visnostic perspective, it is the biggest mistake made today in Corporate America's sales and marketing departments. The chances are high that you will not remember the letters or what order they came in and your clients won't either.

Example – Recently, I was having a conversation with a reader and she kept using the acronym MSA. Coming from the software world, MSA stood for Master Service Agreement so I was having a really difficult time following the points she was making. It wasn't until well into the conversation that I asked what MSA meant in her world and it meant Marketing Specialist Agencies. Visnostics would have really helped our conversation!

One of the most powerful messages Visnostics evangelizes is that we must avoid making our clients TRANSLATE our message. Acronyms force the client to translate what they stand for so we must stop that madness!

From a Visnostic perspective, these three graphics are a better way to help you learn and retain the information. Can you guess the meaning?

RTH =

RESULTS   TIMELINE   HOW

As you learned from the Introduction, Simon Sinek's book, *Start With Why* points out that most marketing messaging starts out with the "What" and "How" companies do things. Instead, messaging should start out with WHY because that is the real reason clients buy.

The Visnostic Statements David created are very good. However if he included results and timelines, they would be GREAT! They are all focused around HOW things are done. This is a natural way we communicate. And I believe it's natural because this approach is rampant in most messaging today.

But I believe the students of Visnostics are going to change that for the better!

I do want to make a very strong point that not all Visnostic Statements are going to have Results and Timelines but the ones that have these components will often end up being your very best ones.

The best way for you to prove this point to yourself is to try some of them with your clients. Write as many as you can and invite your best client to lunch. Ask him or her to respond but to also let you know which ones resonated and triggered the most emotion. Mix in some Visnostics that have results and timelines with the statements that omitted them.

Their reactions to them will validate this claim.

Remember that a Visnostic Statement is not a promise or claim that you can do something. It is a way to help uncover what is important to your client.

Because David is with Randy White Real Estate Services, I decided to go explore randywhite.com. This is something you can do as well to assess your own marketing. Most potential clients are going to do exactly what I'm doing; I'm looking for results and timelines in his client testimonials. I need to "translate" what is on his website. "Why should I care about what is stated on his website." "How is this agency better than the others?" "What is in it for me?"

Results almost always answer these questions and differentiate one company from all the others.

I'm going to paste the first three testimonials I see and demonstrate what to look for when creating the strongest Visnostic Statements.

Example #1 – Read this and look for RESULTS and TIMELINE.

"We have known Randy White for many years and have had the good fortune to have him as our Agent on two separate occasions. Randy is a true professional who knows his business and the market inside and out, and has given us excellent advice always. He and his team, Brenda and Teresa, are great to work with, extremely responsive and are always looking out for our best interests. Aside from the fact that Randy just sold our house quickly and efficiently, this team is a true pleasure to work with. All around it is a win to work with Randy White!"

Here is some additional coaching before you review the other examples:

Because results and timelines are important to clients, they tend to naturally mention them but sometimes you will have to dig for them. In this example, the seller didn't get to the result until the very end of the recommendation. Unfortunately, most people will stop reading before they get to those results. But with some minor coaching, the seller could turn this into a really impactful referral by just moving some words around.

Also remember that we are so conditioned to believe WHAT someone does is a result, that it's normal to overlook the actual RESULT of what they do. For example, "Randy is a true professional" is what he does. "Answering all their questions" is a result of his professional demeanor but it's still something he does. Refer back to the beginning of the book when I described symptoms and causes and how a doctor has to be careful not to attempt to treat a symptom. The Doctor will need to diagnose the cause before he or she can properly treat the patient.

In Visnostics, the thought process is similar; Randy is professional but the result is that he sold their house quickly. He gave excellent advice but the result from that advice is that the house sold quickly. You can give great advice and be professional all day long and still not sell a house. So we can assume that something Randy is doing is more effective than other Real Estate Professionals. We need to flush out what that is to differentiate him from all the other people trying to sell homes. **Visnostics is a thought process because you will begin to view your marketing wording very differently once you learn what clients really care about.**

"...has given us excellent advice" is really what the Agent DID. What resulted from the good advice? Saved money? Sold house faster? Because we aren't making any claims, we are going to take some liberties here to develop a sample statement. However, finding these types of incomplete results and/or timelines is a great excuse to go back to the client and try and flush out these details.

Timeline – "always"
(the more precise timeline given, the better the quality of the Visnostics)

Results mentioned – "Randy sold our house" (efficiently)
Timeline – "quickly"
(It would be nice to know specifically how quickly. Was it a day? Week? Month?)

Example #2 –

"We met Randy White in 1994 and instantly knew we would have a great relationship with him. He has helped us sell and buy three homes since we met him. Randy has always been positive in listing our homes and that they would sell quickly. His extensive knowledge of the real estate business is why we always trusted him in listing our homes. His office personnel are just as positive and knowledgeable as he is. Any questions or concerns were quickly answered by Randy or his assistant. We support and recommend him and his staff to anyone who has real estate needs."

Results mentioned – "sell and buy three homes"
Timeline – "1994...since we met him"

Results mentioned – "they would sell"
Timeline – "quickly"

Example # 3 –

"Randy was wonderful to work with and is very knowledgeable about the metroplex market. His office staff were always easy to speak with and quick to return our phone calls or emails when necessary. The process went as smoothly as it could have in today's uncertain economy."

Results mentioned – this one omitted the results. We can't even tell if this recommendation is from a Buyer or a Seller. It's assumed that their house sold or they bought a home. It was very focused on the "WHAT" they did to make it a good experience versus what were the desired outcome/results.

Timeline – "always" "quick"

So out of the first three recommendations I reviewed, two were fairly strong and one was complimentary but the outcome could be clearer.

VERY IMPORTANT POINT - This Visnostic Statement creation process is a powerful exercise. Looking for results and timelines will open your eyes to why some marketing "feels" better than others.

Are you starting to see how your thought process is already changing? Once you know what to look for, you will view previous recommendations very differently.

Once you embrace the Visnostic Communication Style, you may want to go back to the clients that provided recommendations and ask them to add these additional details. You will find that most people will be eager to make those enhancements for you.

So now let me show you the Visnostic Statements we can create from these three client testimonials:

Always try and start with the RESULTS and then the TIMELINE. You may be surprised how difficult this is to do because of how conditioned we are to start with the HOW in our sentences.

REMEMBER that our attention spans are down to 3 seconds. That means your first three words better be powerful for the reader to even consider continuing with your message. The best way to catch attention is by putting results first.

"I saved a million dollars" is much more powerful when it was saved in a month versus ten years. Which is why including a timeline is very important to include in your statements.

Visnostic Statements from Exercises 1, 2, & 3 above are:

1. **Randy sold two of our homes quickly due to his professionalism, his efficient team, and his knowledge of the industry.**
2. **Randy has helped us buy and sell three homes since 1994 due to his extensive knowledge of the real estate business and his positive and knowledgeable team.**
3. **Not enough information to create a Visnostic Statement. This one just praised his performance. We have no idea if they even sold or bought a home.**

Here is another way to word them and present them. Can you tell which of these are for Sellers and which are for Buyers?

Please choose one of these three responses to each statement below.

- **I can say this today!**
- **I WISH I could say this today!**
  or
- **It's not important, not applicable, or I don't know**

Our Agent <u>sold</u> our house <u>quickly</u>. (Seller)
We <u>saved thousands of dollars</u> thanks to <u>always</u> receiving excellent advice from our Agent. (Unknown)
We have <u>bought or sold three homes</u> in <u>25 years</u> with the same Agent. (Buyer AND Seller)
The entire selling and buying experience was <u>always</u> <u>enjoyable</u> because the entire team was so <u>responsive</u> to our needs. (Buyer AND Seller)

These are very good Visnostic Statements but I went back to the references in an attempt to find a dream recommendation.

I want to create a GREAT Visnostic Statement for this real estate section and I found a really good one that was buried! In fact, this one is so good that if I were Randy, I would put THIS recommendation FIRST on my webpage!

As you read through this recommendation, try and find all the timelines first.

Timelines are usually complementary to a result.

EXAMPLE #4 – Best Source for Visnostic Statements

"We have worked with Randy over the last 15 years or so in all our personal real estate transactions. He has acted as our agent/broker on three different properties of ours. In all cases Randy was always of the utmost integrity, completeness of task, acted in the best interest of all parties, gathered our requirements accurately and never put any unnecessary pressure on us to do something we did not want to do. He is a true professional and I would recommend Randy to anyone I know or don't know. One most important factor I do not want to miss is, his knowledge of the markets, and understanding how to price homes to sell them is outstanding. (IE) In all three transactions where he sold our properties for us he sold them and had a contract on all of them in less than one week when the market was running at 100 days plus to contract. In summary, Randy White is a true professional, and no matter in the future whatever real estate transactions we are involved in, you can count on it that we will be securing Randy White to handle them for us!! "

Timeline – 15 years, in less than one week.
Results – sold our (3) properties
Before I write the Visnostic Statement, I want to point out that there is a ton of positive feedback here. But think like the client, not like an agent. You may find this is extremely difficult to do.

Almost all of these recommendations declared Randy White as a very knowledgeable professional. That is great. However, the potential buyer or seller has to translate that into "Why do I care about this?" "What is the benefit to me?" "Everybody says they are professional so I still don't understand why he is different." YOU MUST DO THIS TRANSLATION FOR YOUR CLIENTS!

The answer they are looking for are usually in the results.

It's also good to differentiate buyer recommendations from seller recommendations because your audience has one of those two things on his or her mind when trying to make a decision. We need to stop making clients do this translation. We must start doing it for them. With that said, here is the GREAT Visnostic Statement I was able to build for this real estate focused book:

My Real Estate Agent had a contract on all three of my homes in less than a week when all the other Agents were averaging 100 days or more!

Did you happen to read the back cover of this book? If so, this may sound familiar. This is so good, I HAD to put it on the cover of this book!

This is a powerful SELLER Visnostic Statement because the reader now knows that the person writing this recommendation was not just a lucky sale; this Agent sold THREE of his homes in less than a week! This recommendation finally did a fantastic job differentiating Randy White from the other agents out there by including the additional information about average sales taking 100 days.

Who wouldn't respond with
"I WISH I COULD SAY THAT TODAY?!"

Conclusion

You should now be able to see how Visnostic Statements can strengthen your marketing content. Remember this post? Can you rewrite this caption using the Visnostic Approach? If not, I am here to help you be successful. Reach out to me on LinkedIn and let's do this together!

3 BEDROOM, 2 BATH HOME AND 30X40 SHOP FOR SALE IN WASHINGTON SCHOOL DISTRICT ON 2.4 ACRES

POSTED ON MAY 28, 2019 BY DEBORAH

Sweet little home that's neat as a pen, on rural acreage with no restrictions! 2.4 acres is fenced on all 3 sides... has a nice 30X40 metal shop with RV hookup, concrete floor, has electric and plumbed for water and sewer. Good production water well and City Water Tap is installed, but not in use. All this in the Washington School District! What are you waiting for!

This mini-lesson, written exclusively for Real Estate Professionals, is intended to give you a taste of what to expect from any of the books in the Visnostic Series.

There are two chapters dedicated to writing incredible Visnostic Statements. This entire book will be included as well. Which is a GOOD thing because repetition increases retention and comprehension! (See Introduction.)

But the major component that is missing from this mini-book is that the full books will teach you how to create actual sales tools that **will ensure new salespeople are confident and competent to interact with clients from their first few days selling!**

To learn more about developing powerful Visnostic Statements, and how to work with your existing clients to create the absolute best testimonials, please read any of the Visnostic Series by Kimberlee Slavik. The books are available in over 42,000 bookstores worldwide.

For information about scheduling workshops or keynote speaking at any of your business meetings, please email info@dynaexec.com.

APPENDIX
Sales Basics Review, Tips, and Answers

neu·ro·sci·ence

ˈn(y)o͞orōˌsīəns/

noun

noun: **neuroscience**; plural noun: **neurosciences**

Any or all of the sciences, such as neurochemistry and experimental psychology, which deal with the structure or function of the nervous system and brain.

Body Language Basics –

> Looking to Their Right = Auditory Thought (Remembering a song)
> Looking to Their Left = Visual Thought (Remembering the color of a dress)
> Looking Down to Their Right = Someone is creating a feeling or sensory memory (Thinking what it would be like to swim in Jell-O)
> Looking Down to Their Left = Someone talking to themselves

Basic Sales Psychology Principles -

Sales rejection is partially due to human natures resistance to being persuaded. Winning a point or argument is what humans want and need.

Good Pain and Bad Pain -

People buy due to pain (GOOD pain is caused by things like rapid growth, lack of resources, supply chain issues, etc. and BAD pain is caused by things like no growth, layoffs necessary, too much stock, etc.) A good salesperson will be attempting to uncover pain throughout the sales process.

Terminology –

B2B – Business to Business – When a company sells to another company.
Example: A computer manufacturer will sell wholesale to a retail store versus the consumer.
B2C – Business to Consumer – When a company sells to the end-user.
Example: When a retail store sells directly to the consumer.
Some companies have distribution models that are both B2B and B2C.

The Art of Answering Questions -

Never ask closed-ended questions – Yes and No answers can be blurted out without any thought behind the answer. Open-ended questions have problems as well because they can go in many different directions and you lose focus on the original intent. Having multiple-choice is the best way for the audience to ponder and consider the options. They have to think harder to answer, which is how you get people emotionally engaged.

Studies have shown that giving people options, triggers chemicals in the brain to choose one. For example – if you say "Will you buy from me?" Yes or No? It is way too easy to say No. However, if you give your client THREE pricing/package options from which to choose, they will typically choose one. So it is an automatic YES. So when I am responded to an RFP (Request for Proposal), RFI

VISNOSTICS – SPECIAL EDITION FOR REAL ESTATE

(Request for Information, or an RFQ (Request for Quotation), I always provide three alternative pricing scenarios. The theory is that they will choose one of the three options vs. eliminating you from the other bids.

Very Important Point –

When a client asks a question, you will automatically want to answer it. Instead, ask what is driving that specific question. Often, the real question is not what the client actually asked. When I go on sales calls with a Software Engineer, Technical Support, Management, or other teammates, their purpose for being on the call is usually to answer all questions sales can't handle. However, when questions arise, it is imperative to uncover what is driving the question so you don't get drug down the wrong path and derail the momentum of the meeting.

For example, I was in a meeting about three weeks before Thanksgiving and the client asked what was the average implementation time. This is a logical question and my engineer wanted to tell the client that the answer was six weeks. Instead of answering the question, I asked the client why this question was important and they responded with they wanted to make sure it could be completed before the holidays (which I just said was in three weeks). If we had answered the question with the "six weeks" response, the client would have jumped to the conclusion that we were not the appropriate solution and we would have lost the sale.

The real question the client wanted to ask was, "Could you have this implemented by the holidays?" And our answer would have been, "Yes, we will double up on resources to ensure implementation is complete by the holidays."

Podcasts and Other URLs:

Visnostic Podcasts, Education, and Speaking:
July 19, 2019 – Donald C. Kelly, The Sales Evangelist
https://www.stitcher.com/podcast/donald-kelly/the-sales-
evangelist-sales-trainingspeakingbusiness-
marketingdonald/e/62674347
June 18, 2019 – Brian Burns of the Brutal Truth About Sales with

Kimberlee Slavik – Basic Visnostics – Statements NOT Questions –

https://www.stitcher.com/podcast/brian-burns/the-brutal-truth-

about-sales-selling/e/61931321?autoplay=true

April 22, 2019 – Dr. Pelè with Kimberlee Slavik – Basic Visnostics -

https://www.youtube.com/watch?v=FbW-sSu4BOo&t=304s

Visnostic Book URL References:
"You Are Who You Are Because Where You Were When"
https://www.youtube.com/watch?v=_aY163kwlW4
"7 Presentation Ideas That Work for Any Topic."
https://www.inc.com/carmine-gallo/7-presentation-ideas-that-
work-for-any-topic.html
Kimberlee Slavik –https://www.linkedin.com/in/kimslavik
Denise Fair - https://www.linkedin.com/in/denise-fair-25768184/
David A. Wiener – https://www.linkedin.com/in/david-a-wiener-
573b1a1/
David's artwork - http://artbydavidwiener.blogspot.com

Neuroscience References:

Using Neuroscience to skyrocket sales

https://neilpatel.com/blog/7-neuroscience-principles-you-should-use-to-increase-sales/

Why Questions and Surveys annoy clients -

https://www.mycustomer.com/community/blogs/wizu/7-reasons-why-your-customers-hate-your-surveys

The Neuroscience of Selling – INC magazine

https://www.inc.com/geoffrey-james/the-neuroscience-of-selling.html

What Great Salespeople Do Summary –

http://storyleaders.com/book/

More Science –

https://blog.insidesales.com/inside-sales-thought-leaders/buyers-brain/

Buy Books:

https://www.amazon.com/Visnostics-VISualization-DiagNOSTIC-Neuroscientific-communicating-ebook/dp/B07T4GB68N/ref=sr_1_1?keywords=visnostic&qid=1562089153&s=gateway&sr=8-1

https://www.amazon.com/Visnostic-Selling-neuroscientific-marketing-leadership/dp/1732191611/ref=sr_1_2?keywords=visnostic&qid=1562089192&s=gateway&sr=8-2

https://www.amazon.com/Kimberlee-Slavik/e/B07NCK2353?ref=sr_ntt_srch_lnk_1&qid=1562089233&sr=8-1

Company and book sites:

www.dynaexec.com
www.visnostics.com
www.visnosticselling.com

WORKSHOPS

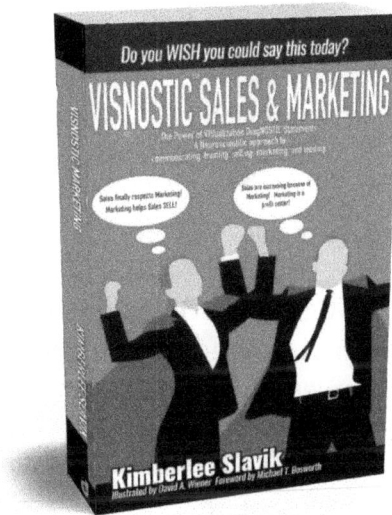

There are three workshops that help DynaExec clients execute three major principles taught in the book. First, all non-client-centric marketing messaging must be translated and converted into client-centric Visnostic Statements. This is accomplished by working with sales and marketing in a *Translation Workshop*. This is the fundamental workshop needed to create stronger messaging. This workshop eliminates the clients need to translate features and functions and other jargon by doing the work for them. This workshop converts current messaging into dialogue that will improve your clients' comprehension and retention of your messaging.

In addition, you will strengthen your rapport with your clients because they will FEEL positive emotions while engaging with your sales organization. Your sales organization will be able to quickly identify the clients' non-strength areas in which your company can convert to strengths.

Once the translation is completed and 10-20 strong "Visnostic Statements" are created, the next step is the **Solution Mapping Workshop**. This second workshop is conducted with a more technical team to review the Visnostic Statements created during the Translation Workshop and get their input.

Often, these second sets of eyes will identify and create additional Visnostic Statements to the ones Sales and Marketing identified during the Translation Workshop. In addition, this second group tend to enhance the newly created statements with powerful results they have observed during their post sales efforts. These final Visnostic Statements are then mapped to various Statement of Work descriptions that will describe HOW any "non-strengths" uncovered during the client discussion can be made into strengths. These Statement of Work descriptions are created during the Solution Mapping Workshop.

The final stage of the Visnostic transformation is to take the Visnostic Statements and the Statement of Works and complete a tool that will be given to the entire sales organization. Imagine a sales team that is in front of the client tablet, documenting the client responses. And residing on the tablet is a tool that will automatically produce an "Insight Report" that will give your clients a recipe for success INSTANTLY!

This will eliminate the need for technical resources to be engaged early in the sales cycle. The client will see exactly how your company will turn their non-strengths into strengths!

The third workshop is **Visnostic Selling**, which is conducted with the entire sales organization to ensure they are each experts with the tool and they are well prepared to properly engage with the client.

Your sales organization will be CONFIDENT and COMPETENT in front of potential clients from their first WEEK in their sales role!

Here are the three workshops in greater detail -

★ Client-Centric Translation For Sales & Marketing

Objective –
Conversion is a form of translation. Converting features and functions into VISualization DiagNOSTIC (aka Visnostic) Statements is the act of translating vendor centric wording (vendor-speak) into client centric statements (client-speak) that clients can relate. DynaExec will assess current marketing tools & combine details from multiple sources to create Visnostic Statements & compatible visuals & graphics that enhance retention.

Attendees –
Sales and Marketing (Up to twelve participants)

Pre-requisites, Planning, and Preparation for Workshop –
- Read Visnostic Selling Book (Preface, Chapters 1-3) Retail Price - $24.95
  Workshop Discounted Rate - $19.95

- **Meeting #1** – Assessment - Conference Call to hear Presentation & Record for transcription (obtain script)
- **Meeting #2** – Assessment Results Revealed. Kick-off conference call after book is read but prior to workshop to set expectations
- **Meeting #3** - Onsite 8-hour Translation Workshop
  - ✓ CHAPTER ONE – Believing is Doing and Introduction (30 minutes)
  - ✓ Exercise #1 – "XXXX" exercise.
  - ✓ Slide presentation using graphics vs words
  - ✓ 3 graphics versus letters exercise – 3 seconds per slide Generation Z get timer added to PPT
  - ✓ CHAPTER TWO – Segmentation and why it is important. (30 minutes)
  - ✓ CHAPTER THREE – Solution Dissection. (1 hour)
  - ✓ CHAPTER FOUR – Translation (1 hour)
  - ✓ CHAPTER FIVE – Creating & Rating Visnostic Statements with Post It Notes by Segmentation. The importance of RTH. Use highlighters to identify, Reword if necessary. Prioritize. (1 hour working lunch)
  - ✓ CHAPTER SIX – Vertical and Target Market Strategies with Visnostic Statements (1 hour)
  - ✓ CHAPTER SEVEN – Class Presentations. Time will be determined based upon number of companies in each session and flexibility of class.
  - ✓ CHAPTER EIGHT – Conclusion and discussion of two additional workshops to create the tool. Demo of tool.

- **Ongoing Meetings (up to 30 days)** –
  Ensure success and document results are included in the workshop price.

Supplies Needed for In-Person Workshop –
- Conference Room with projection and white board
- Phone for call-in participants
- Internet
- Post-it Notes supplied by DynaExec
- Highlighters supplied by DynaExec

★ Mapping Segmentation Solution Workshop for Post Sales Roles

Objective –
After the feedback from the client is collected, a deliverable must be created that maps all "NON-STRENGTHS" identified with Visnostic Statements. It is important to not simply map products or services names to the areas in which can be strengthened. This workshop will summarize HOW your company will help clients improve their current situations. The result will be a client deliverable called an Insight Report.

Attendees –
Technical Team such as Software Engineers, Implementers, Support, Compliance, etc. (Up to twelve participants)

★ Visnostic Sales and Marketing Workshop

Objective –
After the first two workshops, a sales tool will be completed that converted features/functions and other technical jargon into

statements the client can reflect and visualize. Sales will learn how to deliver this approach in lieu of a traditional sales presentation. Sales will learn how to use the new tool designed to create the Client Insight Report. Sales people need to be entertained to learn. This workshop will have games and prizes.

Attendees –
Sales and Sales Leadership (Up to twelve participants)
In less than 30 days and three workshops, with Visnostic Selling, your sales, marketing, and leadership will be transformed into Client Business Strategists. Furthermore, your clients will no longer avoid your teams' sales efforts because they will be viewed as a valuable extension of your client's own teams.

★ Additional Information

Workshops can be conducted in public forums or in private sessions.

The benefit of group forums is that during your presentation to the group, you will be educating other companies on the benefits, results, and differentiators of your company, which could result in new clients.

TIP – Companies that send representatives from both marketing and sales will benefit the most from the Translation Workshop, which is the most popular and fundamental one to strengthen the effectiveness of the messaging.

★ Assessment of Current Messaging – Pricing Options

ASSESSMENT - $1,500
This includes approximately 10 hours of consulting work prior to the in-person workshop. Cost of the Assessment will be applied to any future consulting services and workshops.

1. Read at the minimum, Preface and Chapters 1-3. (2 hours)
2. Record your best presentation (30 min max) on Zoom with slides.
3. Transcribe the presentation. (3 – 5 hours)
4. Bring four different highlighter pens (blue, yellow, pink, and green are preferred).
5. Be prepared to discuss your top five differentiators over your competition. (1 hour of research)
6. Download app – Poll Everywhere

POST WORKSHOP - $500/month retainer for consulting services.

Visnostic Selling Readers and Pod Cast audience may contact podcast@DynaExec.com for *a free assessment ($1,500 value).* *

When was the last time you purchased a $25 book and received $1,500 of consulting for FREE?

*Special Pricing is for a Limited Time Only

BIOGRAPHIES

Author Bio and Resumé

Kimberlee Slavik –
https://www.linkedin.com/in/kimslavik

Kimberlee is an award-winning business strategist in the Information Technology (IT) industry, known for helping clients increase sales and profits by leveraging software, services, hardware, storage, business continuity, & cloud computing.

Currently CEO of DynaExec.
Member of several advisory boards.

Results:
- ✓ Best Selling Author of Visnostic Selling Series
- ✓ Award Winning Global Sales Leader
- ✓ Over 85 unsolicited recommendations on LinkedIn from clients, peers, direct reports, indirect reports, and management validating accomplishments
- ✓ Sold or participated in selling over $1.9 billion worth of software, products, & services during a 30-year career
- ✓ Exceeded $900 million-dollar revenue objectives while managing a complex, 70+ person storage team with P&L accountability for HP
- ✓ Recipient of numerous sales awards by focusing on post-sales support and customer references
- ✓ Exceeded quota for 26 years of a 30-year career averaging almost 200% of plan

Specialties:

- ✓ Surpassing sales objectives
- ✓ Expert Selling Intangible Offerings
- ✓ Excellent Post Sales Client Relationships
- ✓ Member of multiple Advisory Boards
- ✓ Training and education development and execution
- ✓ Transforming sales organizations into top performers
- ✓ Business acumen & P&L (Profit and Loss)
- ✓ 15 years of people leadership
- ✓ Excellent communication & presentation skills
- ✓ Key Note Speaker
- ✓ Collaborative team player leading multiple teams towards a common goal
- ✓ Project management & organizational skills
- ✓ Organizational design & coaching high-performance teams
- ✓ Enterprise channel strategy development & execution
- ✓ C-level executives & senior execs sales closures
- ✓ Indirect enterprise channel sales & marketing
- ✓ Expertise in Technology – including SaaS (Software as a Service), cloud, storage, virtualization, & Business Continuity

Education:

- ✓ Summa Cum Laude from LeTourneau University, with a Bachelor of Science degree in Business Administration.
- ✓ Certified by Southern Methodist University in "Leading the High-Performance Sales Organization."
- ✓ Currently pursuing an MBA degree in International Business at Heriot-Watt Business School in Edinburgh, Scotland.

Foreword Bio and Resumé

Denise Fair - https://www.linkedin.com/in/denise-fair-25768184/

Denise Fair is a licensed Texas REALTOR who is also the owner of RE/MAX Centex in Waco, which she purchased in 2011 and quickly tripled its size in both number of agents and market share.

Not only is she an accomplished and experienced REALTOR, she has also demonstrated her entrepreneurial, management, and people skills by being named RE/MAX of Texas Broker/Owner of the Year in 2012 and again in 2014. RE/MAX Centex is the largest RE/MAX franchise within a 100 mile radius of its Waco, Texas location, and her proven ability to grow and cultivate the sales skills of her agents coupled with her servant heart have made her a notable force in the RE/MAX network and the real estate industry.

Denise offers a perspective to the real estate sales industry that is unique among her colleagues. In addition to being a licensed agent, she serves as Senior Escrow Officer of a title company and has closed tens of thousands of real estate transactions in her long career with her firm. She is recognized as the "go-to" escrow professional in Central Texas for her efficient management of residential, commercial, farm and ranch, short-sale, and tax-free exchange transaction settlements.

She has exploited her dual career path with a proficiency typical of her work ethic, benefitting real estate agents, sellers, buyers, and lenders alike. Moreover, as a paralegal, her proficiency in real estate, agency, and contract law better enables her to work with clients of her companies and other Real Estate Agents from the contractual stage of complex transactions through settlement and disbursement.

Denise is married to real estate attorney Walt Fair. Together they have four brilliant and beautiful daughters, two son-in-laws, and two precious grandchildren. They reside on their ranch in Valley Mills, Texas.

Artist Bio and Resumé

David A. Wiener – https://www.linkedin.com/in/david-a-wiener-573b1a1/

David is an action-oriented generalist with diverse sales and marketing experience in high technology environments. After engineering design and system installation of cryogenic systems, he entered the selling world of investment brokerage of large apartment buildings.

Then, after a decade of real estate investment, he moved to the high-tech industry. He has a strong focus on business start-up, market expansion, and turnaround situations. He demonstrated success in sales and sales management of system and application software as well as hardware. He has been successful at small and large companies and divisions of large companies starting new ventures. He has held positions up to and including VP Sales. He has held a TS clearance and has expertise with systems integrators and government programs.

After his career in high tech, David moved on to small farm communities in Florida, Texas and then upstate New York where he built a studio and produces his art of fine ink drawings, oil paintings, and ceramics. He also spends his time working for his town as chair of the planning board. He also is a member of the County planning board and a board member of the town fire department.

Education: Newark College of Engineering - BSME, MSIE, MSCIS (abt)

For more information about David's artwork or to commission his talent, please visit http://artbydavidwiener.blogspot.com

www.ingramcontent.com/pod-product-compliance
Lightning Source LLC
Chambersburg PA
CBHW062010200326
41519CB00017B/4750